Taoist Cosmic Healing

Chi Kung Color Healing Principles for Detoxification and Rejuvenation

Mantak Chia

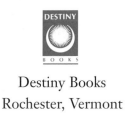

Destiny Books

Rochester, Vermont

Destiny Books
One Park Street
Rochester, Vermont 05767
www.InnerTraditions.com

Destiny Books is a division of Inner Traditions International

Originally published in Thailand in 2001 by Universal Tao Publications under
the title *Cosmic Healing I: Cosmic Chi Kung*

LIBRARY OF CONGRESS CATALOGING-IN-PUBLICATION DATA

Chia, Mantak, 1944-
Taoist cosmic healing : chi kung color healing principles for
detoxification and rejuvenation / Mantak Chia.
p. cm.
Includes bibliographical references and index.
ISBN 978-0-89281-087-1
1. Qi gong. 2. Color—Therapeutic use. 3. Detoxification (Health)
4. Rejuvenation. I. Title.
RA781.8.C4697 2003
615.5'3—dc21
2003010225

Printed and bound in the United States by Versa Press

10   9   8   7   6   5   4   3

Text design by Priscilla Baker
Text layout by Virginia Scott Bowman
This book was typeset in Janson with Present, Futura, and Diotima as
the display typefaces

Contents

Acknowledgments

The Universal Tao Publications staff involved in the preparation and production of *Taoist Cosmic Healing* extends gratitude to the many generations of Taoist masters who have passed on their special lineage, in the form of an oral transmission, over thousands of years. We thank Taoist master I Yun (Yi Eng) for his openness in transmitting the formulas of Taoist Inner Alchemy.

Thanks to Juan Li for the use of his beautiful and visionary paintings illustrating Taoist esoteric practices.

We offer our eternal gratitude to our parents and teachers for their many gifts to us. Remembering them brings joy and satisfaction to our continued efforts in presenting the Universal Tao system. As always, their contribution has been crucial in presenting the concepts and techniques of the Universal Tao.

We wish to thank the thousands of unknown men and women of the Chinese healing arts who developed many of the methods and ideas presented in this book. We also wish to express thanks to Cosmic Healing Certification Retreat organizers around the world who have worked with us for many years helping to prepare this manuscript.

We express special thanks to Sarina Stone for her generous assistance in revising and editing this edition of *Taoist Cosmic Healing*. Thanks also to Nancy Ringer and Vickie Trihy for their editorial expertise. In addition, we wish to thank Colin Campbell, Matt Gluck, Dennis Huntington, Annette Dirksen, and Dirk Oellibrandt for their writing and editorial contributions to the first edition of this book.

We wish to further express our gratitude to all the instructors and students who have offered their time and advice to enhance this system, especially Felix Senn, Barry Spendlove, Chong-Mi Mueller, Clemens Kasa, Andrew Jan, Marga Vianu, Harald Roeder, Salvador March, Dr. Hans Leonhardy, Peter Kontaxakis, Thomas Hicklin, Gianni Dell'Orto, and Walter and Jutta Kellenberger.

We also wish to thank the scientists and testing institutes: Gerhard Eggelsberger, Institute for Applied Biocybernetics Feedback Research, Vienna, Austria; and Dr. Ronda Jessum, Biocybernetics Institute, San Diego, California.

Putting Taoist Cosmic Healing into Practice

The practices described in this book have been used successfully for thousands of years by Taoists trained by personal instruction. Readers should not undertake these practices without receiving personal instruction from a certified instructor of the Universal Tao, because some of these practices, if done improperly, may cause injury or result in health problems. This book is intended to supplement individual training by a Universal Tao instructor and to serve as a reference guide for these practices. Anyone who undertakes these practices on the basis of this book alone does so entirely at his or her own risk. Universal Tao instructors can be located at our websites: www.universal-tao.com or www.taoinstructors.org

The meditations, practices, and techniques described herein are *not* intended to be used as an alternative or substitute for professional medical treatment and care. If a reader is suffering from a mental or emotional disorder, he or she should consult with an appropriate professional health care practitioner or therapist. Such problems should be corrected before one starts training.

This book does not attempt to give any medical diagnosis, treatment, prescription, or remedial recommendation in relation to any human disease, ailment, suffering, or physical condition whatsoever.

Chinese Medicine and Chi Kung emphasize balancing and strengthening the body so that it can heal itself. The meditations, internal exercises, and martial arts of the Universal Tao are basic approaches to this end. Follow the instructions for each exercise carefully, and do not neglect the foundations (such as the Microcosmic Orbit and any other supplemental exercises). Also pay special attention to the warnings and suggestions. People who have high blood pressure, heart disease, or a generally weak condition should proceed cautiously, having received prior consent from a qualified medical practitioner. People with venereal disease should not attempt any practices involving sexual energy until they are free of the condition.

The Universal Tao and its staff and instructors cannot be responsible for the consequences of any practice or misuse of the information in this book. If the reader undertakes any exercise without strictly following the instructions, notes, and warnings, the responsibility must lie solely with the reader.

Taoist Cosmic Healing

Introduction
What Is Cosmic Healing Chi Kung?

Cosmic Healing Chi Kung is an important branch of Universal Tao, a system of Taoist practices for cultivating the body, the Chi, and the spirit. *Chi* means "energy" or "life force"; *kung* means "work." Cosmic Healing Chi Kung is the cultivation of the ability to conduct Chi for the purposes of healing. We call this practice "Cosmic Healing" because we ultimately learn to use the forces of nature, human will, and cosmic particles to transform negativity stored in the body. This discipline can benefit anyone interested in forms of healing that are complementary to Western medicine, either for themselves or as a practitioner; any person who desires a higher level of awareness of the human potential; and any person who wants to heal a physical disorder.

Human beings exist because of the unique combination of the forces that are around and within us. The two main forces are electricity and magnetism. *Bio-electro magnetism* is the Western term for "life force," or what Taoists refer to as Chi. *Bio* signifies life, *electro* refers to the universal energies (yang) of the stars and planets, and the *magnetism* refers to the earth energies (yin) or gravitational force present on all planets and stars. Bio-electro magnetism, or Chi, pervades all of heaven, earth, and nature. For the past five thousand years, practitioners of Cosmic Healing Chi Kung have used time-tested methods to tap into these unlimited reservoirs of Chi, greatly expanding the amount of healing energy available to them.

Human beings contain two types of Chi: Prenatal Chi, which combines Chi and Ching (sexual energy), is inherited from the parents and is visible as innate vitality, and Postnatal Chi, which is the life force an individual cultivates in his or her lifetime and is visible as the light shining behind personality and self-awareness. To build their Postnatal Chi, humans normally access bio-electro-magnetic energy through food and air. Plants take the universal energies of the sun and the magnetic energies of the earth and digest and transform them, thereby making these energies available to all living beings. Rather than connecting to Universal Chi only after it is processed through plants, however, Taoist practitioners of Cosmic Healing Chi Kung go directly to the source of this primordial energy. As we align ourselves with cosmic forces, we become a conduit through which we can absorb and digest these energies through the body, mind, and spirit, establishing a direct connection with the universe. Through Chi Kung and meditation, we are then able to direct this energy of the universe precisely.

Universal Tao views human beings as lamps filled with oil. Many people burn this fuel at very high intensity, without ever taking the time to replenish the oil in the lamp. Alcohol, drugs, tobacco, and promiscuity all quicken the depletion of this fuel. The exercises of Universal Tao strive to refuel the energy within. The Taoist recognizes that human beings have a limited capacity for Chi. However, if we are able to connect with the sources of Chi within the universe, we gain an infinite capacity for Chi, and we constantly fill ourselves, within the limitations of our human nature, with the unlimited abundance of energy around us.

According to Taoist belief, the root of most physical ailments is stuck or stagnating Chi. Practitioners of Cosmic Healing Chi Kung clear these Chi blockages by connecting to earth and universal forces and conducting the stronger, cleaner, more positive energy they provide into the body to move the negative or blocked Chi.

Through their internal quest, the Taoists discovered a doorway to the universe. The more readily we can conduct our internal energy, the more we are capable of conducting the forces of energy around us.

Human beings have amazing potential and capabilities. We are unique creatures in the way we use our minds and hands. Look at the world around us: the skyscrapers, the architecture, the technology, and the myriad creations of man. All have come about through the combination of the mind with the hands. In the Universal Tao practice, we use the mind and the hands, through Chi Kung, to connect to the forces of the universe. We use the mind to project a pattern of energy into the universe, to connect to the force, and to bring this energy back into the body. With the mind and the hands, each of us can journey into the boundless energy of the universe.

> Cosmic Healing Chi Kung works very well with Chi Nei Tsang (internal organ Chi massage), another Universal Tao practice. Cosmic Healing Chi Kung, Chi Nei Tsang, and all the other Universal Tao practices play a unique role in working to heal the physical and subtle bodies. When you combine these practices in synergy, they allow you to perform many healing tasks.

TEACHERS AS STUDENTS

An important part of Cosmic Healing Chi Kung is the cultivation of healing skill to share with the community. True to the Tao, a student of Cosmic Healing Chi Kung begins by learning about the self and facilitating change within. Once the self has been cultivated to a high degree, the student may easily share his or her knowledge with others, becoming in turn the teacher. Thus, in this book the term "student" may refer to either the Chi Kung practitioner or the receiver of Chi Kung. Ultimately, we are all potential students and teachers at any given time.

Self-Preparation
How to Feel and Conduct Chi

MASTERING CHI

One of the most basic foundations of Universal Tao is mastery of Chi. If you cannot control Chi, you cannot practice Cosmic Healing Chi Kung. In Universal Tao, there are five stages to learning to master Chi. Once you have succeeded in one stage, you may move on to the next.

By far, the easiest way to learn these five steps is to train under the supervision of a Universal Tao Certified Instructor. At the time of this book's publication, there are over two thousand certified instructors around the world. Go to www.universal-tao.com and click on the instructor directory to find a qualified instructor near you.

This book alone may help to bring you, the reader, a greater understanding of the principles of this particular form of Chi Kung. However, as has been the case for over five thousand years, the true way of Taoist teaching is through oral transmission. For a complete learning experience, both teacher and text are recommended.

Step 1: Conserve Chi

Our first goal is to learn to conserve our Chi. There are any number of metaphors you can use to visualize this concept: For example, when a battery is totally drained, it is harder to charge; in the same manner, when you are drained of energy, it is harder to regain energy. As another example, you have to have money to make money; in the same manner, you have to have Chi to make Chi.

To have more Chi, we need to maintain control of the gates through which energy normally leaks out and unwittingly drains our life force. We leak energy:

- through our reproductive system
- through negative emotions
- through constantly turning our senses outward

Without knowing how to conserve the Chi that we already have, what is the point of acquiring more?

Step 2: Balance Chi

We next must learn to balance our Chi; that is, we seek to keep a smooth and balanced flow of energy moving throughout the whole body. If our energy is imbalanced, we may have too much energy in some places and not enough in others; we may also be too yang or too yin. We may have excess or deficient heat, cold, damp, or dryness. This imbalanced energy tends to make us go to extremes.

Step 3: Transform Chi

Next we learn to transform our Chi into more beneficial energies. For example, through the Taoist Sexual Chi Kung practices taught in the Universal Tao system, we can transform sexual energy into basic life-force Chi. Through other practices (such as the Inner Smile and the Six Healing Sounds), we learn to transform negative emotional Chi into positive virtuous Chi. Thus Chi is not only the foundation of our health but also the basis of spiritual development.

Step 4: Increase Chi

When we have completed the first three phases of mastering Chi, we then learn to increase it by tapping into the vastness of Universal Chi. It is very important to master the stages of conservation, balance, and transformation before we emphasize increasing our Chi. Otherwise we may waste the energy we bring in, or we may inadvertently amplify the imbalanced or negative energies that we have not yet learned to bring under control.

Step 5: Project Chi

Finally, we learn to extend our mind to tap into the Universal Chi and project that energy to heal our body, mind, and spirit and to heal other people. The practice of Cosmic Healing Chi Kung sensitizes your hands to the feeling and movement of Chi; it uses the mind-eye-heart power to absorb Universal Chi into the palm and crown and to send it out through the hands and beyond, so that you can help restore balance in others without touching them or draining Chi from yourself. (This may sound fantastic, but recent researchers in Chinese Chi Kung hospitals have measured the energies emitted by Chi Kung masters and found them to be of different varieties and frequencies. This research has been corroborated by experiments in the United States at such places as the Menninger Institute.)

MIND, EYE, AND HEART POWER

The opening of the mind, eyes, and heart and the use of intention is vital for further activating and increasing your Chi. In Taoism we achieve this by cultivating our Yi (pronounced "yee"). Yi leads and guides Chi. With our mind we control thought patterns. With our eyes we control the senses of sight, hearing, smell, and taste. With our heart we control all our organs and their related emotions: the kindness/anger of the liver, the joy/impatience of the heart, the openness/worry of the spleen, the courage/sadness of the lungs, and the gentleness/fear of the kidneys. Yi controls all these things. It is mind-eye-heart power melded with our intention.

Every excellent achievement in our lives depends upon the quality and efficient operation of our Yi. Combining the awareness of the mind, eyes,

YI LEADS AND
GUIDES CHI

heart, and intention into one creates a rich and rare alchemical mixture. The power of Yi is the magical catalyst that assures energetic results.

When you have control of Yi, you are inwardly aware of your mind, senses, and heart; you are outwardly aware of the universal energy. Now you are capable of receiving the abundantly available healing power of the universe; you can tune into everything, inwardly and outwardly in all directions. This is what we are here for: to heal and become whole again. We have higher goals to reach. The foundation for reaching our goals is a strong and healthy body.

Cosmic Healing Chi Kung is merely an extension of the universe within yourself. With your Yi, you draw the universe in through your palms, skin, heart, and crown, absorb its power, condense it, transform it, and use it for the benefit of all.

To learn to activate and control Yi, you must master the foundational practices of the Universal Tao system.

THE FOUNDATIONS OF UNIVERSAL TAO

A practitioner's level of skill in Cosmic Healing Chi Kung will be based upon his or her mastery of the Universal Tao system as a whole. One can easily learn the simple movements of Cosmic Healing Chi Kung without doing any other Universal Tao practices. However, if one truly wishes to master the art of Cosmic Healing Chi Kung, it is important to have a firm foundation in the basic Universal Tao practices.

To attain skill in Cosmic Healing Chi Kung, one should know and practice the Universal Tao basic meditations: Cosmic Inner Smile, Six Healing Sounds, Microcosmic Orbit, Iron Shirt Chi Kung, and Healing Love. Most of these practices, being integral to the exercise of Cosmic Healing Chi Kung, are described in this book. Beyond this basic level, the Universal Tao System offers many other intermediate and advanced Chi Kung practices and meditations. The further one advances, the greater one's mastery of Chi. Your increasing level of skill in the Universal Tao system will reflect immediately in your Cosmic Healing Chi Kung practice. Furthermore, you will discover that you can incorporate many of your Universal Tao practices directly into your practice of Cosmic Healing Chi Kung.

Once you have learned the basic meditations of Universal Tao, you can begin the unique preparatory practice for Cosmic Healing Chi Kung. The preparatory practice consists of a few parts; work through each part at your own pace and eventually join them together as a whole. Always start with Warm Up the Stove at the abdomen and direct the fire down to the sexual center to transform the sexual energy. Next practice Cosmic Inner Smile, followed by Bone Breathing, Marrow Washing, and Microcosmic Orbit.

Warm Up the Stove

This exercise teaches you to activate the Chi of your Lower Tan Tien, a reservoir of energy in the lower abdomen. (See chapter 2 for more information about the Tan Tiens.) It also allows you to transform potent sexual energy to Chi.

1. Sit on the edge of a chair with your hands clasped together and your eyes closed.
2. Begin "bellows breathing," moving your abdomen in and out quickly. Emphasize the exhalation by breathing out forcefully. Take eighteen to thirty-six breaths in this manner. Then rest for a moment, covering your navel and feeling nice and warm.
3. Begin "inner laughing," as if you were attempting to contain laughter, so that you feel your abdomen vibrate on the inside. Practice this for a few minutes, allowing the movement of your inner laughter to grow stronger.
4. Rest now, and use the mind-eye-heart power to gather Chi (now felt as a warmth behind the navel) into the Lower Tan Tien. Picture the Tan Tien as a stove with burning fire behind your navel. Feel nice and warm.
5. Once the Tan Tien is warm, smile down toward it and the sexual organs, and feel the warm or fiery Chi flow from the navel area to the sexual organs. Women should bring the Chi down to the uterus, and men should bring the Chi down to the testicles. Feel the Chi as sun shining on the water; the rays of the sun purify the water until it becomes rising steam. This transforms sexual energy into Chi, and this Chi rises up the spine into the brain, helping to activate the crown and mideyebrow energy centers.
6. Focus your awareness in the sacrum. At the very tip of the sacrum is a hole, called the sacral hiatus, in the coccyx. Breathe into this hole until you feel some activity—perhaps a tingling, numbness, or pulsing—there. Activating this point will generate suction. Feel the suction force

pulling Chi through the sacral hiatus into the body; breathe into it until you feel it become activated. When the sacrum is activated, you will feel the suction easily, as well as breathing in the cranium and mideyebrow. Keep gently smiling and softly breathing into the Lower Tan Tien and feeling the suction into the abdomen from the sacrum. Focus 95 percent of your awareness in the Lower Tan Tien and 5 percent in the sacrum, the crown, and the mideyebrow. Be aware of the Lower Tan Tien breathing and observe internally the pulsing and breathing in the sacrum, the mideyebrow, and the crown. Breath in this manner thirty-six times.

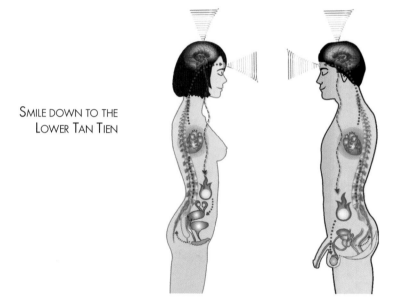

SMILE DOWN TO THE
LOWER TAN TIEN

Cosmic Inner Smile

The Cosmic Inner Smile is a powerful relaxation and self-healing technique that uses the energy of love, happiness, kindness, and gentleness as a language to communicate with the internal organs of the body. Each organ corresponds to a specific element and color. For example, the kidneys correspond to the element of water and the color blue, while the heart corresponds to the element of fire and the color red. Using the appropriate color or element, one can guide healing power into each organ.

ORGAN	COLOR	ELEMENT
Heart	Red	Fire
Lungs	White (or pink)	Metal
Liver	Green	Wood
Kidneys	Blue	Water
Spleen	Yellow	Earth

The practice also aids the transformation of negative emotions into positive virtuous energy. This transformation is a very powerful Chi Kung practice. A genuine smile transforms negative energy into loving energy that has the power to relax, balance, and heal. By learning to smile inwardly to the organs and glands, you will cause your whole body to feel loved and appreciated and to enjoy more Chi.

The Inner Smile begins at the eyes and the mideyebrow point and moves down to the heart. As you activate the heart, loving energy will flow out and you will feel the energy of your Inner Smile flow down the entire length of your body like a waterfall. This is a very powerful and effective tool to counteract stress, tension, and negative Chi.

1. Focusing your awareness on the mideyebrow, close your eyes and imagine that you are in one of your favorite places in the world, a place where you feel safe, relaxed, and happy. Recall the sights you saw there, the sounds you heard, and the scents, sensations, and flavors you associate with that place.
2. Imagine that one of your favorite people is standing in front of you, smiling to you with loving, happy, radiant, shining eyes. Smile to your own face, slightly lifting up the corners of your mouth.
3. Feel yourself responding to that special person's smile with a smile of your own. Feel your eyes smiling and relaxing.
4. Smile down to the thymus gland and picture a white flower blossoming. Gently inhale into the thymus gland, connecting your breath to the olfactory organ. Smell the good fragrance.
5. Aim your inner attention at your heart. Picture the heart before your inner eye and smile to it. Smile until you feel the heart smile back to you. Picture your heart like a red rose, gradually opening. This will activate the love and fire of compassion in the heart. The heart's red light

and loving awareness will, in turn, activate the cosmic red healing light or mist from above and around you.

6. Smile at the red light or mist and very slowly, with a soft, long, deep breath, draw the red mist, love, and compassion into the mideyebrow, down through the mouth and throat, and into the heart, where it gradually overflows to the small intestine. Retaining the red light and the love and compassion in the heart and small intestine, exhale the cloudy black or negative energy. Repeat this breathing eighteen to thirty-six times, or until the heart becomes bright red before your inner vision and starts to radiate loving red light out to the tongue, mouth, nose, ears, and eyes.

RED FOR THE HEART
WHITE FOR THE LUNGS
YELLOW FOR THE SPLEEN
BLUE FOR THE KIDNEYS
GREEN FOR THE LIVER

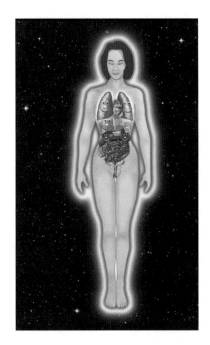

INNER SMILE

Allow the red light to whirl around you and form a red aura. Feel your skin glowing with red energy.

7. Let the heart's loving energy radiate out to the lungs. Aim your attention at the lungs; picture them before your inner eye and smile to them. Smile until you feel the lungs smile back to you. Picture your lungs like a white rose, gradually opening; smell the good fragrance. This will activate the courage in the lungs. Once you invoke the white light and courage to shine from within the lungs, you will also activate the cosmic white healing light or mist from above and around you.

8. Smile at the white light or mist and very slowly, with a soft, long, deep breath, draw the white mist into the mideyebrow, down through the mouth and throat, and into the lungs, where it gradually overflows into

the large intestine. Retaining the white light and the feeling of courage in the lungs, exhale the cloudy black or negative energy. Repeat this breathing eighteen to thirty-six times, or until the lungs become bright white and start to radiate the white light of courage out to the nose, ears, eyes, tongue, and mouth. Invite the white light to whirl around you and form a white aura covering your skin like autumn dew.

9. The spleen, pancreas, and stomach correspond to the yellow color of the earth element. Aim your attention at these organs; picture them before your inner eye, and smile to them. Smile until you feel them smile back to you. First connect to the heart. The heart is the root of compassion, and it is always a good idea to take a moment and connect with the heart and feel its connection to the other organs. Picture the spleen center as a yellow rose, slowly opening and radiating a yellow light. This will activate the cosmic yellow healing light or mist from above and around you. You might see the golden yellow aura of a wheat field ready for harvest.

10. Smile at the yellow light or mist and very slowly, with a soft, long, deep breath, draw it into the mideyebrow, down through the mouth and throat, and into the spleen center. Fill the spleen center with the golden yellow light. Exhaling, expel feelings of worry and the cloudy, sticky energy. Repeat this breathing eighteen to thirty-six times. Then allow the light to radiate out to your mouth, nose, ears, eyes, and tongue. Wrap the golden aura around you, leaving a golden shine on your skin.

11. The kidneys and bladder correspond to the blue color of the water element. Aim your attention at these organs; picture them before your inner eye, and smile to them. Smile until you feel them smiling back to you. Picture the kidneys as a blue rose, slowly opening. See them radiate the blue healing light of gentleness. Once you've invoked the blue light of the kidneys, you will also activate the blue cosmic light above and around you.

12. Smile at the blue light or mist around you and very slowly, with a soft, long, deep breath, draw it into the mideyebrow, down through the mouth and throat, and into the kidneys. Retaining the blue light and the feeling of gentleness, exhale, expelling feelings of fear or stress and the cloudy or negative energy. Repeat eighteen to thirty-six times, or until the blue light of gentleness starts to radiate out from your kidneys to your ears, eyes, tongue, mouth, and nose. Gather the blue mist on your skin, enveloping yourself in a blue aura.

13. The liver and gallbladder correspond to the green color of the element wood. Focus your attention on these organs; picture them before your

inner eye and smile to them. Smile until you feel them smile back at you. Picture them as a green rose, slowly opening and radiating green healing light of kindness. Once you've invoked the green light of the liver and gall-bladder, you will also activate the green cosmic light above and around you.

14. Smile at the green light or mist around you and very slowly, with a soft, long, deep breath, draw it into the mideyebrow, down through the mouth and throat, and into the liver and gallbladder. Retaining the green light and the feeling of kindness, exhale, expelling the dark red cloudy heat of anger. Inhale the nourishing green of the forests, inviting in kindness. Repeat eighteen to thirty-six times, or until the green light has completely filled the liver and starts to radiate out to your eyes, tongue, mouth, nose, and ears. Invite the green light to form a green aura around you.

15. Smile down to the sexual organs and reproductive system. Smile until you feel them smile back to you. Feel the heart (love) and sexual organs (arousal) uniting. Observe how this process transforms sexual energy into Chi. Now imagine this Chi as a beautiful, gentle pink color that radiates from your sexual organs. Thank the sexual organs for their work in keeping you alive and healthy. Rest. Do nothing. Gather and store the energy by smiling and use your mind to "spiral" the energy to the Lower Tan Tien. (Spiraling is a way to condense Chi in an area so that it may be stored.)

Microcosmic Orbit

I began my practice of Chi Kung when I was a child. After many years of practice with many Chi Kung forms, I started to forget the first form, so I learned it again. One day when I tried to practice and review all the forms that I had learned, I couldn't remember many of them. I sat down and thought, "I only have two hands, two legs, and one head. Why are there so many forms to remember?" I said to myself that there must be one main thing that they all have in common. I started to search, and I found out that the most important thing is feeling the Chi within us, and being able to increase, transform, take in, and stay in touch with the universal, cosmic, nature, and earth forces.

Many people, including some Chi Kung masters, have come to me and said that they have been practicing Chi Kung for years but they don't feel any energy. They think that they must be performing their Chi Kung incorrectly. I tell them that the hand movements of the Chi Kung forms are nothing by themselves. There are hundreds of different Chi Kung forms in China. You could spend seventy lifetimes just learning the hand movements. But if you do not also practice meditation, your Chi Kung suffers.

The practice of Microcosmic Orbit meditation will help you to feel Chi more easily inside, outside, and around the body. It awakens, circulates, and directs Chi through two important energy routes in the body: the Governor Channel, which ascends from the base of the spine up to the head, and the Functional Channel, which runs from the tip of the tongue down the middle of the torso to the perineum. Microcosmic Orbit also strengthens Original Chi and teaches you the basics of circulating Chi. It allows the palms, the soles of the feet, the mideyebrow point, and the crown to open. These specific locations are the major points where energy can be absorbed, condensed, and transformed into fresh new life force. Dedicated practice of this ancient esoteric method eliminates stress and nervous tension, energizes the internal organs, restores health to damaged tissue, and builds a strong sense of personal well-being.

Microcosmic Orbit meditation is the foundation of Cosmic Healing Chi Kung. Your Chi Kung practice is dependent upon the quality of your meditations and your ability to perfect the Microcosmic Orbit. In order to master Cosmic Healing Chi Kung, you must practice this meditation daily.

1. Focus on the Lower Tan Tien (the area where the Original Chi is stored, between the navel, kidneys, and sexual organs). Feel the pulsing in this area, and observe whether this area feels tense or relaxed, cool or warm, expansive or contracting. Notice any sensations of Chi: tingling, heat, expansiveness, pulsations, electric or magnetic sensations. Allow these to grow and expand. Let the Chi of the Lower Tan Tien flow out to the navel.

2. Use your mind-eye-heart power (Yi) to spiral the Chi in the navel point, guiding and moving it. Let the energy flow down to the sexual center (the ovaries for women, or the testicles for men).

3. Move the energy from the sexual center to the perineum and then down to the soles of the feet.

4. Draw the energy up from the soles of the feet to the perineum and then to the sacrum.

5. Draw the energy up from the sacrum to the Door of Life (the point in the spine opposite the navel).

6. Draw the energy up to the mid-spine point (the T-11 vertebra).

7. Draw the energy up to the base of the skull (also known as the Jade Pillow).

8. Draw the energy up to the crown.

9. Move the energy down from the crown to the mideyebrow point.

10. Touch the tip of your tongue to your upper palate; press and release a

few times. Then lightly touch the palate with the tongue and leave it there, sensing the electric or tingling feeling in the tip of the tongue. Move the energy down from the mideyebrow to where the tip of your tongue and the palate meet.

11. Move the energy down from the palate through your tongue to the throat center.

12. Move the energy down from the throat to the heart center.

13. Bring the energy down from the heart to the solar plexus. Feel a small sun shining out.

14. Bring the energy back down to the navel.

15. Continue to circulate your energy through this sequence of points, making at least nine cycles. Once the pathways are open, you can let your energy flow continuously like a river, without needing to stop at each point.

16. When you are ready to conclude the exercise, collect the energy at your navel.

> **Men:** Cover your navel with both palms, left hand over right. Collect and mentally spiral the energy outward from the navel thirty-six times clockwise and then inward twenty-four times counterclockwise.
>
> **Women:** Cover your navel with both palms, right hand over left. Collect and mentally spiral the energy outward from the navel thirty-six times counterclockwise and then inward twenty-four times clockwise.

Six Healing Sounds

Everyone has heard stories about gifted beings who possess great healing powers. People seek out these gifted healers. Yet even in the best of circumstances, how much time can a great healer spend with you? One hour a day? One hour a week? What happens the rest of the time?

For optimal health, you must learn how to take care of yourself; you must learn how to clear out your negative energy and transform it to positive healthy energy. Maintaining yourself in this way will surely enhance any other therapy you are receiving.

The Six Healing Sounds practice is a simple yet powerful tool to promote physical, energetic, and emotional healing and balance. Regular daily practice of the Six Healing Sounds will help you keep in touch with the energetic and emotional state of your internal organs. Practice this exercise in the evening before you go to sleep. By clearing out negative emotions before sleeping, you allow the night's rest to recharge your energy positively. This practice will greatly benefit your personal Cosmic Healing Chi Kung practice. It will help sensitize you to the varieties and differing qualities of Chi. This knowledge will also help you in diagnosing and treating others. If you are healing others, you can teach them one or two of the Six Healing Sounds each session to enhance the effects of your therapeutic work.

The sounds are used to generate certain frequencies for specific healing. Each sound can generate different energy for the healing of different organs. Growing the good virtue of the organs is essential so that the negative or sick energy has less room to grow.

Once the movements, sounds, and information have been integrated into your practice, you can simplify and make the Six Healing Sounds more powerful. For example, when you are settled into the lung sound and you are breathing white healing light and feel the mideyebrow wide open, you can bring your awareness to the Tan Tien and the universe. Chi will flow from the universe into the Tan Tien, and just the right amount and quality of Chi will flow from the Tan Tien into the lungs and large intestine. This technique works for any of the healing sounds; just set up the location (the organ) and connect to the universe, and Chi will flow to the correct location.

When practicing the Six Healing Sounds, keep your eyes open only while making each sound. Take a deep breath and smile to the organ between each healing sound exhalation.

For more details of this practice, see the book *Taoist Ways to Transform Stress into Vitality* by Mantak Chia.

Lung Sound

Element: Metal
Associated Organ: Large intestine
Sound: *Sssssss* (tongue behind the teeth)
Emotions: Negative—grief, sadness, depression
Positive—courage, righteousness, high self-esteem
Color: White, clear, metallic
Season: Fall
Direction: West

LUNG SOUND

Position: Sit in a chair with your back straight and your hands resting palms up on your thighs. Have your feet flat on the floor about hips' width apart. Smile down to your lungs and be aware of any sadness, grief, or excess heat in your lungs. Slowly inhale, and raise your hands up your center line, with your fingers pointing toward each other. When your hands pass shoulder level, begin to rotate the palms out as you continue raising your hands in front of you and above your head, with the palms up. Point your fingers toward the fingers of the opposite hand and keep your elbows slightly bent.

Sound: Part your lips slightly, holding your jaw gently closed. Look up through the space between your two hands and push your palms slightly upward as you slowly exhale and make the sound *sssssss*. Picture and feel any excess heat, sadness, grief, depression, sickness, or dingy white color expelled and released as you exhale slowly and fully.

Resting Posture: When you have completely exhaled, rotate the palms to face downward with the fingers still pointing toward each other. Slowly lower the palms and bring them just in front of the chest, feeling the lungs' aura.

Close your eyes and be aware of your lungs. Smile into your lungs, and as you inhale, imagine that you are breathing in a bright white mist of light. Breathe this light into your lungs and feel it cooling, cleansing, invigorating, healing, and refreshing your lungs. Feel it flowing down to the large intestine to balance the energy of the yin lungs and yang large intestine, allowing the courage quality of your lungs to emerge. Grow more courage so that sadness and depression have less room to grow. With each inbreath, feel yourself drawing in cool fresh energy. With each outbreath, mentally make the lung sound and release any remaining sadness or hot energy.

Repeat at least three times. For the first two repetitions, make the sound aloud. On the third or last repetition, make the sound subvocally (so softly that only you can hear it). To alleviate extreme sadness, depression, cold, flu, toothache, asthma, or emphysema, repeat six, nine, twelve, or twenty-four times.

Kidney Sound

Element: Water
Associated Organ: Bladder
Sound: *Chooooo* (with your lips forming an
    "O" as if blowing out a candle)
Emotions: Negative—fear, shock
Positive—gentleness, wisdom
Color: Dark blue or black
Season: Winter
Direction: North

Position: Move your hands to cover the

KIDNEY SOUND

kidneys. Smile to your kidneys, and be aware of any excess cold or heat in the kidney region. Then bring your legs together, ankles and knees touching. Lean forward and clasp the fingers of both hands together around your knees. Inhale, and pull your arms straight from the lower back while bending the torso forward (this allows your back to protrude in the area of the kidneys). Tilt your head upward as you look straight ahead, still pulling on your arms from the lower back. Feel your spine pulling against your knees.

Sound: Round the lips slightly and slowly exhale while making the sound *chooooo*. Simultaneously contract your abdomen, pulling it in toward your kidneys. Imagine any fear, sickness, imbalances, excess cold, or excess heat energy being released and squeezed out of the fascia surrounding the kidneys.

Resting Posture: After you have fully exhaled, slowly straighten until you are erect and return your hands to touch the aura of the kidneys. Close your eyes and again be aware of your kidneys. Smile to your kidneys, and on the inbreath, imagine you are breathing a brilliant luminous blue light mist into them. Feel this mist healing, balancing, and refreshing your kidneys and bladder, and picture them glowing a bright blue color. On the outbreath, imagine you are still making the kidney sound.

Repeat at least three times. Repeat six, nine, twelve, or twenty-four times to alleviate extreme fear, fatigue, low-pitched ringing in the ears, dizziness, back pain, bladder or urinary infection, or problems of the reproductive system.

Liver Sound

Element: Wood
Associated Organ: Gallbladder
Sound: *Shhhhh*
Emotions: Negative—anger,
    frustration, resentment
Positive—loving kindness,
    benevolence, forgiveness
Color: Green
Season: Spring
Direction: East

Position: Place your hands over the liver. Smile to your liver, and be aware of any anger, frustration, resentment, or excess heat in the liver region. Slowly begin to

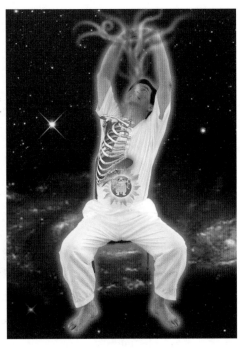

LIVER SOUND

inhale a deep breath as you extend your arms up from the sides with your palms up. Raise your palms over your head. Interlace your fingers together and turn your joined hands over to face the sky, palms up. Push out through the heels of the palms and extend the arms up, keeping the shoulders relaxed. Bend a little to the left and stretch your right arm slightly to gently open the area of your liver.

Sound: Open your eyes wide (the eyes are the sensory opening of the liver). Slowly exhale, making the sound *shhhhh* subvocally. Feel that you are releasing any trapped excess heat, anger, illness, or negativity from your liver and that these are riding out of your body on your breath.

Resting Posture: Once you have fully exhaled, close your eyes, separate your hands, turn the palms down, and slowly lower your arms to the sides, leading with the heels of the hands. Smile, and inhale a shiny spring green mist, illuminating the liver and gallbladder. Bring your hands back to rest on the liver's aura. Close your eyes and smile into your liver. With each inbreath, breathe fresh Chi into your liver and gallbladder. With each outbreath, mentally make the liver sound.

Repeat at least three times. Repeat six, nine, twelve, or twenty-four times to alleviate extreme anger, to relieve red or watery eyes, to remove a sour or bitter taste in the mouth, or to detoxify the liver.

Heart Sound

Element: Fire
Associated Organ: Small
    intestine
Sound: *Haaaaaw*
Emotions: Negative—
    arrogance, harshness,
    cruelty, hatred
Positive—joy, honor, respect,
    love, happiness
Color: Red
Season: Summer
Direction: South

Position: Let both hands rest on the heart. Smile to your heart,

HEART SOUND

and be aware of any arrogance, haughtiness, hatred, giddiness, cruelty, or hastiness in it. Slowly begin to inhale a deep breath as you extend your arms up from the sides with your palms up, as you did with the liver sound. Raise your palms over your head. Interlace your fingers together and turn your clasped hands over to face the sky, palms up. Push out through the heels of the palms and extend the arms up, keeping the shoulders relaxed. Bend a little to the right and stretch your left arm slightly to open the area of your heart.

Sound: Keeping your eyes soft and relaxed, look up through your hands. Slowly exhale, making the sound *haaaaaw* subvocally. Feel that you are releasing any trapped heat, negative emotions, illness, or imbalance from your heart and that these are riding out of the body on your breath.

Resting Posture: Once you have fully exhaled, close your eyes, separate your hands, turn the palms down, and slowly lower your arms to the sides, leading with the heels of the hands. As you move, inhale a bright red mist into the heart and small intestine. Bring your hands back to rest on your heart's aura. Smile into your heart. With each inbreath, breathe fresh Chi into your heart. With each outbreath, mentally repeat the heart sound.

Repeat at least three times. Repeat six, nine, twelve, or twenty-four times to alleviate extreme impatience, hastiness, arrogance, nervousness, moodiness, jumpiness, irritability, tongue ulcers, palpitations, sore throat, heart disease, or insomnia and to detoxify the heart.

Spleen Sound

Element: Earth

Associated Organ: Pancreas, stomach

Sound: *Whooooo* (gutturally from the throat)

Emotions: Negative—worry, excess sympathy, overthinking

Positive—fairness, balance, equanimity, justice, openness

Color: Yellow

Season: Indian summer

Direction: Center (where you stand, looking out to the Six Directions)

SPLEEN SOUND

Position: Place your hands on the body so that they cover the spleen, pancreas, and stomach area. Be aware of your spleen, and smile sincerely into it. Inhale deeply as you move your arms outward in an embrace, and aim the fingers up under the left rib cage.

Place the fingers of both hands just beneath the sternum and rib cage on the left side.

Sound: Look out, lean into your fingers, and gently push your fingertips in. Exhale slowly and make the sound *whooooo* from the depths of your throat. Feel yourself releasing any trapped heat, worry, mental fixations, or excess sympathy.

Resting Posture: Once you have fully exhaled, close your eyes, slowly release the hands, and extend your arms out, embracing the earth. Return your hands to the resting position on the spleen's aura. Smile to your spleen, pancreas, and stomach. With each inbreath, inhale fresh Chi to your spleen, pancreas, and stomach as a brilliant luminous yellow healing mist that cleanses and refreshes your organs. With each outbreath, mentally make the spleen sound.

Repeat at least three times. Repeat six, nine, twelve, or twenty-four times to alleviate extreme indigestion, heat or cold in the stomach or spleen, worry, nausea, hemorrhoids, fatigue, organ prolapse, or loose stools.

Triple Warmer Sound

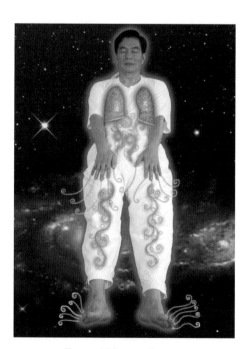

TRIPLER WARMER SOUND

The term *Triple Warmer* refers to the upper, middle, and lower torso and to the distinct metabolic transformations that occur within each area. The Upper Warmer is the area above the diaphragm, where the heart and lungs are located. This area tends to become hot and is responsible for respiration and cardiovascular circulation. The Middle Warmer, the area between the diaphragm and the navel, becomes warm and is where the digestive organs are located. The Lower Warmer, the area below the navel, is responsible for reproduction and elimination and is cool in temperature. The sound *heeeee* balances the temperatures of the three levels by bringing hot energy down to the lower center and cold energy up to the higher centers.

Position: Lie on your back with your arms resting at your sides, palms up. Keep your eyes closed. Smile. With a single inhalation, breath first into the upper part of your lungs to expand the Upper Warmer, then into the middle of the lungs to expand the Middle Warmer, and finally into the lower lungs to fill the Lower Warmer. Breathing in this way creates more space inside the torso for each organ, helping to release and circulate any internal heat or cold.

Sound: Exhale while making the sound *heeeee* subvocally, flattening first your chest, then your solar plexus, and finally your lower abdomen. Feel the dark and cloudy color and the cold energy exit from the tips of the fingers.

Resting Posture: Once you have fully exhaled, do not focus on any emotions or purification process. Instead, just let go and relax your body and mind completely.

Repeat at least three times. Repeat six, nine, twelve, or twenty-four times to alleviate insomnia and stress.

❂

When you have completed the Six Healing Sounds, just rest, smile, and do nothing.

Smile to Connect with the Universe Within

Paradoxically, in order to project ourselves out into the immensity of the galaxies and the universe to gather limitless resources of Universal Chi for healing, we must first journey within ourselves. In order to "go out," we must first "go in." The vehicle for this magical journey is powered by our ability to relax in mind and body. As we physically relax, letting go of muscular and emotional tensions and joint and bone structures, and turn on our very special subtle smile, we gain access to the inner realms. We open the pathways of the parasympathetic nervous system. This helps us reduce the outflowing habits of our senses so that we can be more alert in sensing our inner universe.

This exercise teaches us to smile to the mideyebrow, eyebrows, eyes, mouth, jaw, tongue, lips, cheeks, ears, shoulders, rib cage, and brain and then to let the observing mind (the upper brain) sink down into the Lower Tan Tien. Practice this exercise until you become familiar and comfortable with it.

1. Smile to the mideyebrow. Relax and let go. Smile to the eyebrows, and let them grow long to the sides. Lower these relaxed sensations down to the Lower Tan Tien.

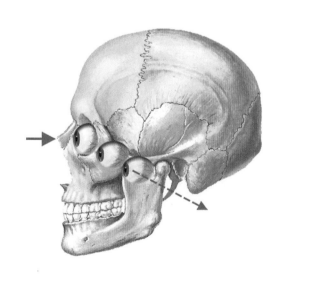

2. Smile to the eyes. Relax the eyes and feel how nice and cool they are. Let the eyes draw back in their sockets and start to sink down to the chest and gradually down to the abdomen, the home of your feeling and awareness mind.

3. Relax the two broad muscles extending from the outer portions of the upper lips across the cheekbones. Lightly smile, feeling the muscles' connection to the upper front of the ears. Gradually feel the ears growing long (up and down). Feel the ears grow all the way down and connect to the kidneys.

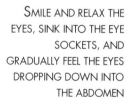

SMILE AND RELAX THE
EYES, SINK INTO THE EYE
SOCKETS, AND
GRADUALLY FEEL THE EYES
DROPPING DOWN INTO
THE ABDOMEN

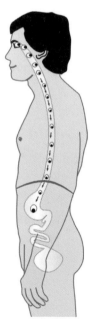

*Self-
Preparation*

4. Open your mouth and relax your jaw, separating the upper and lower teeth. Feel the jaw relax. Once the jaw relaxes, the shoulders will relax and drop down. Continue to feel the jaw relax until you feel saliva start

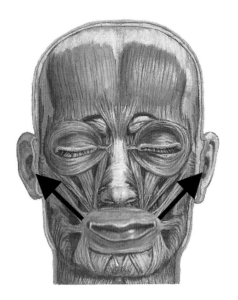

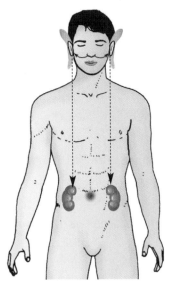

to come out. Relax down to the rib cage. Feel the rib cage drop down, softening all the joints, relaxing down to the Lower Tan Tien. Let the tongue relax back in the mouth. Feel the tongue start to drop down into the throat to the chest and all the way down to the navel, sinking the "floating" sensation down to the Lower Tan Tien.

5. Smile to the shoulders. Relax until you feel the shoulders drop and the rib cage relax.

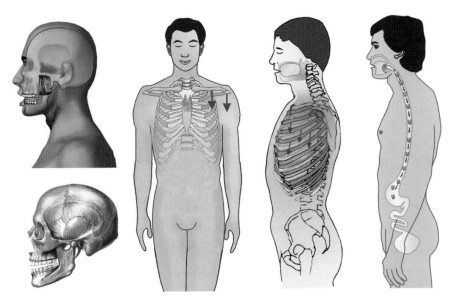

SLIGHTLY OPEN THE MOUTH AND SMILE DOWN TO THE JAW. RELAX THE JAW, AND THE SHOULDERS AND TONGUE WILL RELAX DOWN TO LOWER TAN TIEN.

Self-Preparation

6. Lightly close the lips, but keep the teeth slightly separated. Physically begin a childlike smile, with the corners of the mouth gently uplifted and the outer edges of the eyes softly crinkled up. Breathe through your nose.

7. Smile into the brain and empty the upper (observing) mind into the Lower Tan Tien.

8. Become aware of your inner universe as a big empty space. Keep on sinking down, into the darkness of your empty space. Keep sinking, and experience the vastness until you get closer and closer to the center, the "original force." Stay relaxed and alert so as to be able to see one dot of light. It becomes a galaxy spiraling inside you.

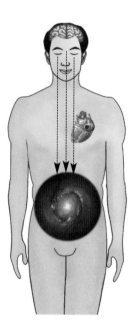

BRING THE SENSES DOWN TO THE LOWER TAN TIEN

True Breath: Skin Breathing

Our bodies are nourished by both physical food and the unique combination of forces that surround us. Our daily caloric requirement is about 6,000 units. We receive only about 2,000 calories from food. The other 4,000 calories come from the forces around, above, and below us: electricity, magnetism, cosmic particle energy, light, sound, and heat. If we don't know how to absorb and transform this cosmic food, we have to depend on others to supply us; we have to ask a priest, monk, or holy person to give us our daily spiritual food.

The Taoists discovered that we can learn to absorb these surrounding and universal energies through the skin and the major energy centers. Absorbing energy through the skin is called the True Breath. This powerful energetic technique requires the Cosmic Inner Smile and relaxation. The more we can relax, the more the body and the skin can open to the energy around us. The practice allows us to extend the mind, to touch the force, and to draw that energy back into the body.

Bone Breathing

Bone Breathing is one of the main practices of Cosmic Healing Chi Kung. The bones and joints of the body have the ability to store Universal Chi to be used by the body. The Bone Breathing process uses the mind and the eyes to absorb Chi into the bones and joints. The practice also strengthens the body so you can hold a higher energetic charge, which is a prerequisite for handling the greater amounts of energy needed for Cosmic Healing Chi Kung. The better your Bone Breathing is, the better your Cosmic Healing Chi Kung practice will be. You will be able to absorb external Chi effortlessly, so you will not need to use your own energy in your healing work.

This method of drawing external Chi through the skin into the bones also helps replenish the bone marrow, thereby reactivating the production of white blood cells. Sending Chi into the bones will enhance functioning of the immune system. This process also helps to clean out fat in the bone marrow ("Washing the Marrow"), one of the main causes of osteoporosis (brittleness of the bones). Tension in the muscles close to the bones is decreased so Chi and blood can flow into the bones easily, enabling them to become stronger.

There are several variations of the Bone Breathing process. Here we will introduce you to the first type of Bone Breathing, inhaling and exhaling Chi through the skin and packing it into the bones. In this method, you imagine that your bones are like hollow tubes, and that you breathe and suck the Chi into the bones. Let your breathing follow a normal pace. Do not strain or hold your breath for too long.

1. You can do this practice in the sitting position (on the edge of a chair, feet flat on the ground, back straight) or any Iron Shirt Chi Kung posture. Using your mind-eye-heart power, breathe in a short breath and at the same time feel suction in your hands. Suck into your hands the Chi of the atmosphere and then of the universe, and breathe in a few more times. Taking small sips of breath, use mind-eye-heart power (Yi) to suck the Chi from the atmosphere into your hands. Once you can clearly feel the increase of Chi pressure in your hands, extend the feeling through your arms. The entire skin surface of the arms breathes in the Chi; feel your skin holding this pressure.

2. Inhale one deep breath and then lightly contract the arm muscles to squeeze the Chi into the bones. Hold the breath and the muscle contraction for a moment to condense the Chi into the marrow of your bones. Then exhale. Upon exhalation you should feel a distinct heaviness in the bones, meaning that the Chi has been condensed and packed into the bones successfully. (As you become more practiced with this exercise, you will learn to use more Yi, less muscle, and softer breathing to draw Chi into the bones.) Repeat six to nine times. Then rest and feel the Chi that has been condensed into the bones.

3. Practicing the same technique you used for your arms, breathe in progressively through the bones of the forearms, upper arms, scapulae, collarbone, sternum, and ribs. The breathing progresses cumulatively; after breathing to the forearms, you'll next breathe to the forearms and the upper arms, and then to the forearms, upper arms, and scapulae, and so on. You may feel a different sensation as you breathe in each area, depending on the bone structure and quality of the marrow. In some areas the feeling is cool, while in others it is warm or tingling.

4. Inhale and exhale in the same way through the toes, feet, and legs. Then, in a step-by-step progression, breathe up through the calf bones, thighbones, pelvis, coccyx, sacrum, and the spinal column to seventh cervical vertebra (C7). As with the arms and upper body, progress from structure to structure cumulatively.

5. Finally, breathe in through the arms and legs simultaneously. Combine

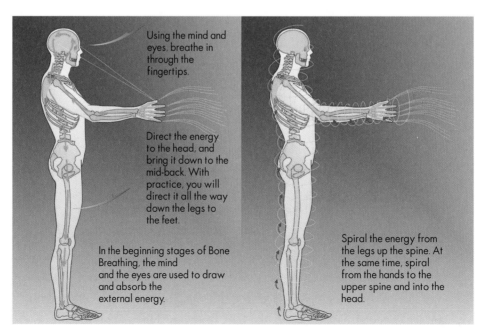

Using the mind and eyes, breathe in through the fingertips.

Direct the energy to the head, and bring it down to the mid-back. With practice, you will direct it all the way down the legs to the feet.

In the beginning stages of Bone Breathing, the mind and the eyes are used to draw and absorb the external energy.

Spiral the energy from the legs up the spine. At the same time, spiral from the hands to the upper spine and into the head.

their energy as it flows up past C7 and up through the neck and skull. Imagine the whole skeleton is breathing, expanding and contracting as a unit. Breathe in this way for at least nine breaths.

6. Conclude by collecting energy at the navel.

Marrow Washing

You can wash your bone marrow with earth force, universal force, or cosmic (man) force. These energies help cleanse and rejuvenate the bone marrow. Specific techniques attain different results. Now, we'll explore Marrow Washing with universal force and violet light.

1. **Men:** Place the left palm on the top of the head, and cover it with the right palm. Bring your awareness to your Personal Star (the star that appears in your mind's eye and is located just above your crown) above you. Lightly press the palms and move them in a clockwise spiraling pattern to the right ear, then to the back of the head and then to the left ear. Repeat nine times in a row, and then rest and feel the increased Chi pressure in the crown. Do three sets.

   Women: Place the right palm on the top of the head, and cover it with the left palm. Bring your awareness to your Personal Star above you. Lightly press the palms and move them in a counterclockwise spiraling

SCOOPING UP THE NORTH STAR AND THE BIG DIPPER

pattern to the left ear, then to the back of the head, and then to the right ear. Repeat nine times in a row, and then rest and feel the increased Chi pressure in the crown. Do three sets.

2. Face your palms toward the heavens and feel that you are scooping a galactic Chi ball from above. This Chi ball contains the North Star (violet) and the Big Dipper (red). See the dipper fill with violet-red energy. Imagine you reach out your arms to hold the dipper handle and pour the violet-red liquid over your crown. You will feel a numbness descending. Face your palms down toward your crown and pour the whole galaxy onto your crown. You may perceive this energy as violet amethyst and red light frequencies. Smile.

3. Guide the sensation of liquidlike Chi down into your skull; deep into your brain, cervical vertebrae, sternum, thoracic vertebrae, and lumbar vertebrae; and down through your legs. Feel it enlivening your bones, penetrating deep into the bone marrow, washing, cleansing, and energizing. The Chi spills all the way down to your feet. Feel it connecting with the earth through the soles of your feet; be aware of the Bubbling Springs point in the feet breathing and pulsating.

4. Touch your navel with the fingers of both hands. Focus on the Door of Life (the point in the spine opposite the navel, also known as Governor Vessel 4), and let the energy activate in the Lower Tan Tien and kidneys. Chi will rise up to the brain.

5. Move your hands down to touch your femur bones. Feel your hands penetrate into the bone and into the bone marrow. Feel a tingling sen-

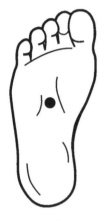

BUBBLING SPRINGS
POINT

CHI SPIRALS LIKE
THE GALAXIES

Self-
Preparation

sation, like that of an electric shock, moving all the way down through the bones of the leg and down to the soles of your feet.

6. Slowly move your fingers down your legs, touching the bone and bone marrow as you go, until you touch the earth. Extend yourself down past the earth to touch the galaxy on the other side. Raise your sacrum and picture yellow light or Chi coming up from the earth and the other side of the galaxy. Focus on the Lower Tan Tien and feel it fill with Chi. Do this visualization three times. Go back down to the squatting position.

7. Place your palms facedown on the earth and be aware of the galaxy and the yellow light. Make three to six circles with your hands to gather the yellow Chi from below. Touch your heels and feel the yellow Chi flowing up the leg bones. Feel the bubbling of your bones as the Chi passes like an electric current up through the feet, tibia, and fibula, femur, pelvis, and spine. Touching your bone and bone marrow with your fingers, slide your hands up along the back of your legs; slowly come all the way up to touch the coccyx and the sacrum. Concentrate on your sexual center so the energy will flow and spread out to the sexual organs. Bring your hands to your navel and gather the Chi into the Lower Tan Tien.

GATHERING
EARTH CHI

The Three Tan Tiens
Connecting to the Powers of the Universe

TAN TIEN ENERGY

Energy in the body can be generated, stored, and transformed by the brain, the sexual organs, and other body organs. However, each of these energy processors is limited in function in some way. The brain, for example, can access and generate energy, but storing energy in the brain is not easy. In the Taoist system, we learn to train the brain to increase its ability and capacity to store energy. The brain energy, when increased to a certain level, can enable more synapses to grow in the central nervous system and can help turn protein into brain and nerve cells.

The organs of the body have a greater capacity than the brain for storing and transforming energy, but their ability to generate energy is limited. The sexual organs, on the other hand, can generate a significant amount of sexual energy (life force). However, the sexual organs cannot store the energy efficiently. When they generate too much energy, considerable amounts have to be discarded. It is like preparing food for one hundred people when only one person is eating. And this "creative" food is the best energy a human has.

As reservoirs of energy in the body, the Tan Tiens bring balance to the body's energy cycle. There are three: the Upper Tan Tien, the Middle Tan Tien, and the Lower Tan Tien. Each Tan Tien is a place where we can store, transform, and collect energy. The Three Tan Tiens feed energy to the meridians, the rivers of energy that flow through the body.

The Middle Tan Tien, also known as the Heart Center Tan Tien, is

THE UPPER TAN TIEN IS IN THE BRAIN, AND WHEN IT IS FULL OF ENERGY, THE CAPACITY OF THE BRAIN INCREASES. WE STORE OUR SPIRITUAL INTELLIGENCE, OR THE MIND, HERE.

located between the two nipples. It is associated with the fire element. Yet within fire there is always water. The original spirit (Shen) is stored here.

The Lower Tan Tien is in the lower abdomen, at the navel. It is like an empty universe or ocean, and we want to feel a universe of energy here. Within this universe or ocean, there is fire under water, like a volcano under the ocean.

The aim of Taoist basic training is to integrate the brain, the sexual organs, the other organs of the body, and the Three Tan Tiens into one system. If the brain generates too much energy, it can store the energy in the organs. If the sexual organs generate excess sexual energy, it can be stored in the organs and the Three Tan Tiens. Without this integration, we waste energy at an alarming rate. Energy is like money. If you make a million dollars a year and spend a million dollars a year, you have nothing left to use in the future. This is the way we live and use energy in our society. We are spending more energy than we are saving, and we are living on borrowed energy, paying very high interest. Our credit will run out very soon.

Some healing practices deal only with the spirit and ignore the body and sexual energy. These practices can generate a lot of energy, but if the practitioner is not connected to the organs, that energy cannot be stored anywhere and is lost. Some people practice meditation by sitting quietly, emptying the mind, and relaxing the whole body. However, very little energy is actually generated in this type of practice. Some who get deep into this type of practice find it hard to come back to society, because they have no energy and their mind power does not work well. These people have to depend on others to support them.

In the Universal Tao, we learn to create a sacred and holy temple within

Taoist practice teaches us that we have a physical body, a mental (mind) body, and a spirit body. We will not explore the spirit body here, but know that it is merely a concept of oneself that is a part of the mind and physical body.

ourselves. With the simple practice of smiling to all the organs, we can begin to integrate our physical, mental, and spirit bodies for future practices. When these bodies begin to integrate, we become more aware of all aspects of the self.

Another important part of that self-knowledge can come from the sexual practice, which connects the mind with the sexual organs. The separation between these parts of ourselves is bridged and a synergy is created. Cultivation of sexual energy is an important part of Cosmic Healing Chi Kung, and a Universal Tao instructor may include practices to cultivate sexual energy in basic instruction. (For more information about sexual energy, consult *Taoist Secrets of Love: Cultivating Male Sexual Energy* and *Healing Love through the Tao: Cultivating Female Sexual Energy*, both by Mantak Chia.)

The Taoist practice provides us with the resources to extend beyond the realm of our senses. By tapping into our internal resources and channeling the energy around us, we can perceive much more than the senses normally report to the mind. We extend our perception from the limited perspective of the sociologically conditioned senses to the unlimited awareness of the universe. For example, our senses tell us that the earth is flat, that we are stationary, and that heaven is above us. In reality, the earth is a sphere hurtling through space at thousands of miles per hour and the heavens are above, below, and beyond the earth in every direction.

The goal of opening the Three Tan Tiens to the Six Directions is to connect with the forces from the six directions—above, below, left, right, front, and back—and draw these forces into the body. In doing so, we learn to continually fill and replenish the energy of the Tan Tiens. Eventually, with practice, we can learn to draw upon many different energies and use them as needed, thereby giving form to the formless energy that is abundant in nature.

TAN TIEN CONSCIOUSNESS

There is a long-standing Taoist practice of cultivating and training consciousness in the Three Tan Tiens, especially the Lower Tan Tien. The consciousness of each Tan Tien is named after its unique focus:

- The Upper Tan Tien corresponds to the *upper* or *observing mind.*
- The Middle Tan Tien corresponds to the *conscious mind of the heart.*
- The Lower Tan Tien corresponds to the *feeling and awareness mind.*

The concept of having multiple brains in the body may seem incredible or far-fetched to some. However, my own experience while participating in scientific research as well as information revealed through recent scientific studies combine to make this aspect of Cosmic Healing plausible, accessible, and practical.

Second Brain Consciousness

Through my participation in several brain wave studies, I came to understand a few simple concepts that are important to Universal Tao, and that's what I am going to share with you. It started in 1994, when Dr. Rhonda Jessum, a clinical psychologist in Los Angeles, asked me to undergo some brain-wave testing. I agreed. The machines at that time didn't tell us much, but it was discovered that when I did the Cosmic Inner Smile meditation, my brain waves went down dramatically, while at the same time my beta waves increased to a very high level. In other words, my higher functions were such that I could drive a car, but my brain was at what was considered a resting and sleeping stage. The puzzled researchers asked, "Hey, how did you do that?" At that time, I didn't know.

After that, I was invited to start testing with the Institute for Applied Biocybernetics and Feedback Research in Vienna, Austria, which is one of the biggest institutes for training top athletes in Europe. Researchers there have developed an instrument that can measure the brain's potential energy, which represents all the energy in the body. The researchers said that their findings prove to the West that Chi exists, that there is energy and a life force running in the body. Their instrument also determines how much energy a person has for the whole day and how much of that energy is for mental clarity and body power.

With the researchers watching and measuring, I did the Cosmic Inner Smile, smiling into my abdomen. They picked up the brain wave readings quickly and said, "Your brain waves are going lower, lower, and resting—and you are nearly in the sleeping state." At the same time, my muscle tension, heart rate, and skin resistance were all very low. Then I surged the energy up from my abdomen to my brain, and the researchers started to see that the energy actually charged up there. They were quite amazed and said, "Hey, this is what we're looking for!"

They asked me what I was doing, and I said, "I'm smiling to my abdomen." They kept on talking to me and asking me questions. They discovered that my observing brain (in the head) was not very active; it was still in a very light resting state. But then how could I answer their questions? They said, "Hey, look! Master Chia is talking to us in his sleep. How can he talk to us in his sleep?"

At last I began to understand. A constant injunction of Taoist practice is "Train the second brain in order to use the second brain." The first (observing) brain and the second (feeling and awareness) brain are linked, and both can carry our consciousness. The second brain charges the observing brain with energy, either purposefully, such as when I surged energy from my Lower Tan Tien up to the Upper Tan Tien, or by default, when by having consciousness in the second brain we allow the first brain to rest. Perhaps it will be easier to understand the first brain and second brain relationship if we call the first brain the "logical" brain and the second brain the "intuitive" brain. The gut, or intuitive brain, receives important messages about our bodies and the world outside and passes these messages to our logical brain. When we strive to listen effectively to our intuitive brain with our logical brain, the result is a better connection to ourselves.

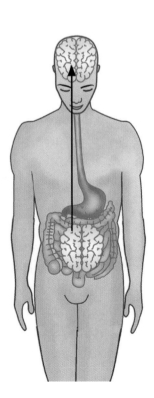

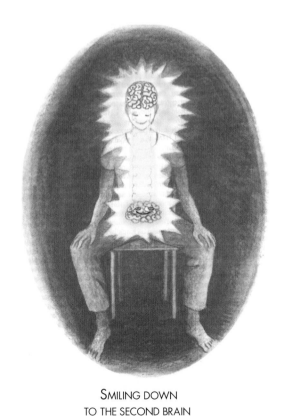

SMILING DOWN
TO THE SECOND BRAIN

ULTRASLOW BRAIN
POTENTIALS
MEASUREMENT
WHILE IN VIENNA

The existence of the feeling and awareness brain has since been proven. In 1996 an article about the "hidden brain in the gut" was published in the *New York Times*. It described the work of researchers who had found that the gut, or enteric nervous system, as they called it, functioned similarly to the brain. They had discovered that the large and small intestines had the same type of neurons as are found in the brain, and that the gut can send and receive impulses, record experience, and respond to emotions. In other words, the gut functioned very much like a brain. Soon after, a book on the subject, called *The Second Brain*, was published.

The *Times* article posed the question, "Can the gut learn?" A Taoist would respond with an emphatic yes. Almost five thousand years of Tao prac-

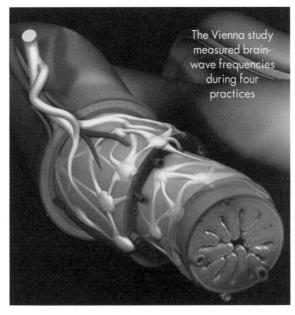

The Vienna study measured brain-wave frequencies during four practices

CROSS-SECTION OF
THE NEURONS IN THE LARGE INTESTINE

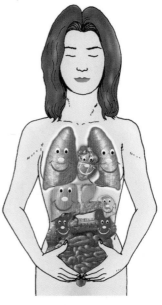

COSMIC
INNER SMILE

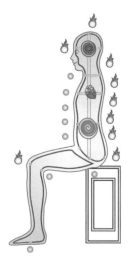

COSMIC ORBIT

SIX HEALING SOUNDS

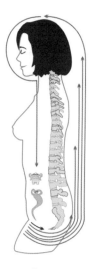

ORGASMIC
UPWARD DRAW

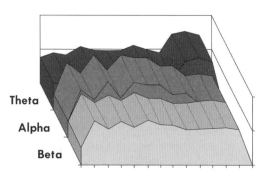

Theta

Alpha

Beta

COSMIC INNER SMILE meditation: THE
ALPHA AND THETA WAVES INCREASE

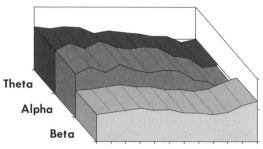

Theta

Alpha

Beta

COSMIC ORBIT meditation: THE ALPHA AND
THETA WAVES HAVE ALTERNATING DOMINANCE

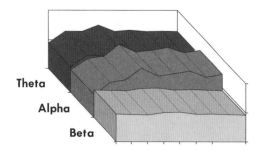

Theta

Alpha

Beta

COSMIC HEALING SOUNDS meditation:
THE ALPHA AND THETA FREQUENCIES INCREASE.
THERE ARE MINIMAL BETA BRAIN WAVES; THE
BRAIN REACHES A STATE OF STILLNESS AND
INTERNAL FOCUS.

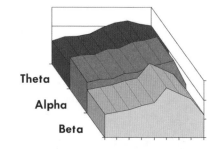

Theta

Alpha

Beta

ORGASMIC UPWARD DRAW meditation:
THE ALPHA AND THETA LEVELS INCREASE

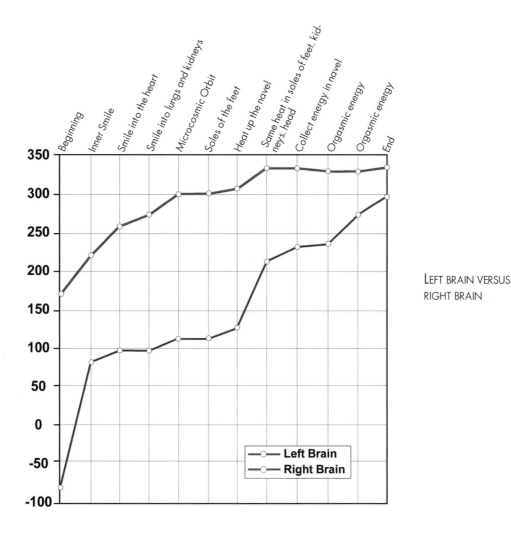

LEFT BRAIN VERSUS RIGHT BRAIN

tice has taught us that we must train all the organs to do different things. In this way, we can use the gut as our conscious brain and allow the head brain to rest. Why is this important? Because the head brain is a "monkey mind," riddled with doubt, shame, guilt, and suspicion. It is always thinking, planning, or worrying. Most people just think and think and think. Scientists have discovered that when people spend a lot of time worrying, their upper (in the head) brain uses a lot of energy. They say that the upper brain can use up to 80 percent of the body's energy, leaving only 20 percent for the organs.

We need to use the brain in the head in order to perform complex functions such as reasoning, making plans, and making calculations. These are typical left-brain functions. However, for our daily life of consciousness, awareness, and feeling, which is typically governed by the right brain, we can use either the brain in the head or the brain in the gut. When we use the upper brain less, it becomes charged with energy and its power increases, and as a result more

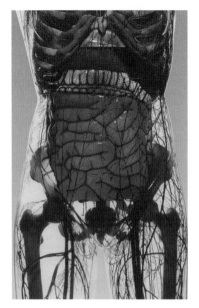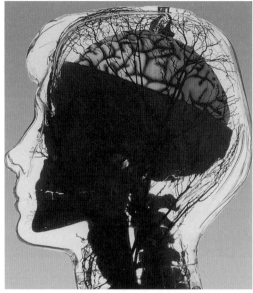

WHEN YOU ARE NOT USING THE UPPER BRAIN, ALLOW IT TO REST BY SENDING CONSCIOUSNESS DOWN TO THE LOWER TAN TIEN

power is available to the body. When the upper brain is resting, brain repair and maintenance occur, and new brain cells can grow. This is the reason Taoism insists that we train the feeling and awareness brain in the gut—so that we can use it when the upper brain is resting. With more charging of the upper brain, we have more power for creativity or whatever we want to use it for. If we like, we can use it to develop our higher spiritual nature.

Consider it this way: For the same job, the head brain charges you eighty dollars, while the gut brain charges you only twenty dollars. So, which one do you want to use? Of course we are not silly enough to choose the overpriced package when we can have the same-quality work done for less cost. But in terms of our own conscious life, we don't know how to choose the more cost-efficient package. We always use the high-priced upper brain. Even worse, we continue using it and using it, until the brain energy is completely consumed. At a certain point, the brain—and concurrently, the body and spirit—becomes empty of energy.

Whenever I smile down, the brain waves in my upper brain decrease very quickly, and the transformed energy from the Lower Tan Tien and organs charges the upper brain. By just flexing the facial muscles into the position of a genuine smile, we can produce the same effects on the nervous system that normally go with a natural spontaneous smile. We can actually make ourselves relaxed and happy by taking advantage of this built-in human mecha-

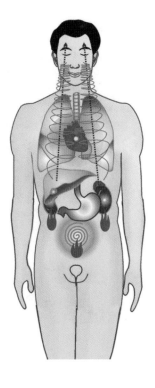

nism. It's natural. Just do it! Learning to smile down to the abdominal area and maintain an awareness of the relaxed, smiling sensation in the Lower Tan Tien is the first step in training the second brain.

Remember these rules:

1. *Empty your mind down to the Lower Tan Tien, and fill the Lower Tan Tien with Chi.* Where the mind goes, the Chi follows.
2. *When your mind is empty, it will be filled.* When the organs have extra energy, that extra energy will rise up and fill the brain with Chi.

The Conscious Mind of the Heart

Taosim considers the Middle Tan Tien, or heart center, also to have its own consciousness, and this belief has recently begun to be proved by medical science. Paul Pearsall's 1996 book, *The Heart's Code*, contains amazing stories of heart transplant patients who found they began to take on some of the preferences, emotions, and even memories of their heart donor. In one case, the donor was a girl who had been killed brutally by an unknown assailant. The recipient of the heart, another girl, started to have nightmares and described somebody killing her. Then she described how the killer looked. Finally the mother took the girl to a psychiatrist, and he in turn contacted the police.

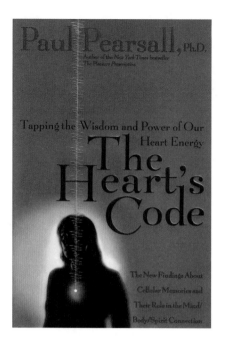

The girl gave the police an exact description of the killer she saw in her dreams, and a police artist drew a likeness of him. With the information provided by the girl, the police were able to find the man. When confronted with clear details of the crime, he confessed to it. From that experience and others like it, medical scientists and others came to realize that the heart, like the upper brain, can record and play back events.

ACHIEVING AWARENESS AND NOT-AWARENESS

Opening the Three Tan Tiens to the Six Directions (the universe all around us) is one of the many resources the Taoist practitioner uses to connect with the universe. The practice combines the power of the mind with the extension of Chi, which allows our personal consciousness to connect directly to the patterns and matrices of energy in the universe. When we put our thoughts into the web of the universe, we transform its electromagnetic energy into a force that is accessible to us. The combination of mind power and energy allows us to establish a relationship to these creative forces and the high sources of energy.

Like some religions and spiritual paths, Taoism places great emphasis on surrender, letting go, and emptiness. This is actually a form of relaxation. When we are relaxed, our muscles are open, our breathing is soft, and energy can flow through the channels of our body. There is no resistance and no fighting. This allows the creative and higher forces to flow into us.

To practice opening the Three Tan Tiens to the Six Directions—to contact and become one with the higher self and the higher forces—you must let go and surrender. Through the surrender of control, you open up and touch the forces of nature. However, if you continue to surrender and let go, you will lose the energy you have sent out. In the long term, this will gradually drain you. The force will suck the energy out of you, rather than help you bring the energy into yourself. To avoid this, at the moment that you are in touch with the higher forces, you must again become aware of yourself and your own energy. You are then able to project your own thoughts, intentions, and patterns into the force, integrating the outer with the doubling or tripling inner energies. You can bring this force back to your place, your house, and yourself.

The idea that you must surrender yourself while using your intentions, mind, and Chi to draw the energy into yourself may seem a paradox. However, as you do the practice and learn how to be empty and open and simultaneously to retain enough consciousness to draw the force into yourself, the paradox will resolve itself and you will see the possibilities it enables.

WARM-UP EXERCISES

These warm-up exercises are designed to be done at the onset of any practice and will wake you up and open the body's energetic channels. Although preparatory in this context, these practices may be done any time you feel the need to wake up and focus.

Rotating the Sacrum

Rotating the sacrum is an excellent exercise to open the lower back and activate the spinal cord. This movement activates the sacral pump.

1. Place one hand over the sacrum and the other over the pubic bone.
2. Rotate the sacrum in a circle thirty-six times in each direction.

Spinal Cord Breathing

This movement activates the cranial and sacral pumps, and loosens all the joints in the spine.

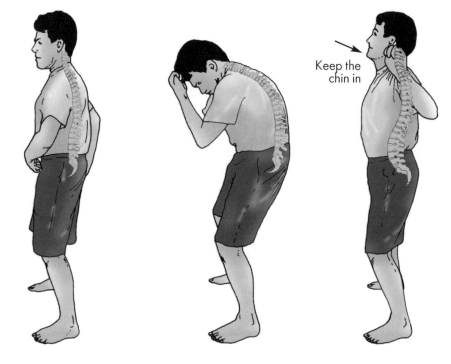

Keep the chin in

ROTATING THE SACRUM   SPINAL CORD BREATHING

1. Inhale and expand the chest, with your arms bent at the elbows and extended to the sides of the body. Keep your chin tucked in toward your throat.
2. Exhale, tucking your tailbone under you, rounding your back, and bringing your elbows toward one another in front of the chest. Smile.
3. Repeat the inhalation and exhalation thirty-six times.

Shaking

Yin and yang are the negative and positive electric forces in the universe. The heart produces positive impulses (the yang electric); the sexual organs produce sexual energy (the yin electric). When we shake the body with a mindful purpose, we loosen stuck Chi and activate our organs and glands, thus assisting in their production of vital hormones. When we concentrate on shaking the sexual organs and on the heart and the mind, we can make the yin and the yang electricity combine. By combining these electrical influences, we achieve new, balanced electricity within ourselves.

1. Shake the whole body loose, especially the joints, by bouncing up and down on your heels. Let all the joints open and relax.

2. Shake the testicles and the breasts loose. This will open the sexual energy (the yin electric).

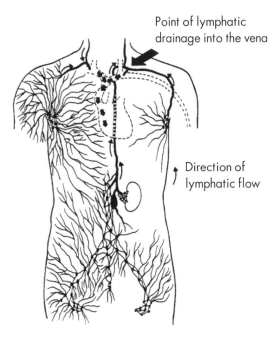

Point of lymphatic drainage into the vena

Direction of lymphatic flow

WHOLE-BODY SHAKING AND THE LYMPHATIC SYSTEM

THREE MINDS INTO ONE: YI POWER

When the three minds (the observing mind, heart mind, and feeling and awareness mind) merge into one, they become the Yi power. Once you are able to achieve this three-mind power, you will be able to activate the six directions and the three fires.

1. Smile into your heart. Make it feel soft. Make it feel love, joy, happiness, and compassion. Feel the heart energy spiral.
2. Spiral the energy in the upper mind. Lower your upper mind down to the Lower Tan Tien in your navel area.
3. Turn the consciousness in your heart, activated by your love and softness, down to the Lower Tan Tien.
4. With the feeling and awareness mind, spiral together the energy of the three minds, blending them together as one in the Lower Tan Tien.

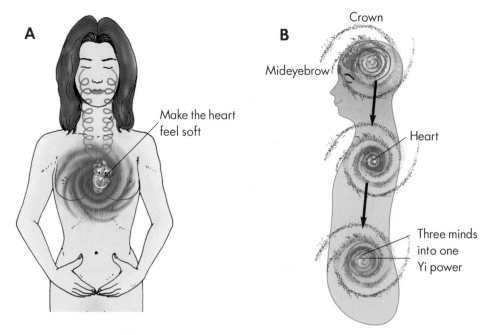

A. The heart softens like a rose blossoming.
B. Spiral the Upper Tan Tien into the Lower Tan Tien and three-mind Yi power.

ACTIVATING THE SIX DIRECTIONS
AND THE THREE FIRES

This powerful energetic technique allows one to extend the mind in the six directions—above, below, left, right, front, and back—to touch the universal forces and to draw that energy back into the body. It also activates and connects the three fires: the Tan Tien Fire, the Kidney (Adrenal) Fire, and the Heart Fire. These are not, of course, real fires; instead, they are Taoist guides to be used for visualization during meditation.

Activating the Six Directions and the Three Fires teaches you how to expand your mind and Chi for receiving healing power. By practicing this exercise daily, you will increase your healing and cosmic power.

Stage 1: Direction Below

1. Spiral the three minds into one.
2. Stand with your feet together. Press your hands down, parallel to the ground. Picture yourself standing on the earth. Smiling into the ground, expand your hands and mind far away, deep down into the earth, beyond the earth, down through the galaxy on the other side, way beyond to the primordial force. It's as if you were extending all the

way to the primordial force that existed 30 million years ago.

3. Push, moving the hands forward six inches only. Connect with the galaxy below.

4. Pull, moving your hands back by your sides. Think about your Lower Tan Tien filling with the Chi of the primordial force. Smile to your Tan Tien, dark, deep and vast. It's as if, with the push, you went to a vast empty space, and with the pull you come back to your Tan Tien, which is also empty and vast, just like the primordial condition before existence. This is where all the forces come from.

5. Push. Touch the primordial force in the universe.

6. Pull. Bring back to your Tan Tien the dark primordial forces with your hands.

7. Keep pushing and pulling until you have performed three to nine times repetitions.

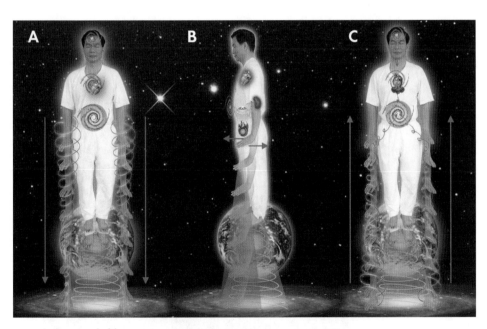

A. HANDS EXPAND THROUGH THE EARTH TO THE GALAXY BELOW.
B. HANDS PUSH FORWARD AND PULL BACK.
C. SMILE TO THE PRIMORDIAL CHI FROM THE UNIVERSE BACK TO THE
LOWER TAN TIEN, AND FILL THE TAN TIEN WITH CHI.

Stage 2: Front Direction and Tan Tien Fire

1. Visualize a small dot of light inside you. Expand your awareness, smiling to the universe in front of you.

2. Become aware of a big fireball in front of you. Feel your hand become

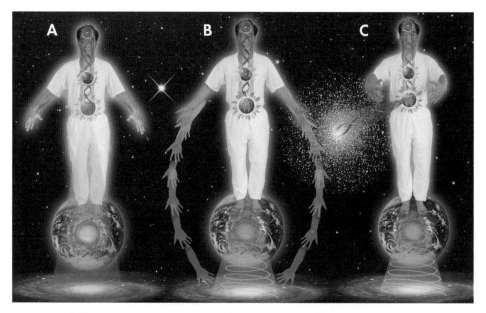

A. Be aware of the universe in front of you. B. Expand your hands to the universe in front, so that they are very big and long. C. Hold the fireball to activate the Tan Tien Fire

Smile to the burning fire

bigger and longer. Scoop up the fireball. You may close your eyes to help your inner sensing.

3. Use the fireball to light the fire in your Lower Tan Tien. Feel the Tan Tien Fire burning in the darkness, the "fire burning under the sea."

Stage 3: Back Direction and Kidney Fire

1. Expand your awareness to the back of your Lower Tan Tien, to the Door of Life, and then farther away. Move your arms toward the universe behind you.
2. Touch the universe. Become aware of the fire of the universe behind you. Scoop up the fire, and use it to activate the Kidney Fire.
3. Maintain your awareness in the Lower Tan Tien and expand, smiling, out to the universe. The energetic spiral glows in the Tan Tien. Spiral in the heart, spiral in your crown, and spiral in the universe.

BE AWARE OF THE BACK DIRECTION, MOVE THE ARMS TOWARD THE BACK OF THE UNIVERSE, AND SCOOP UP THE UNIVERSAL FIRE

Stage 4: Heart Fire

1. Lifting your elbows to the side, raise your hands up under your armpits. Feel yourself holding two fireballs.
2. Feel your fingers extending deep into your body from the side. Touch your heart. Activate the Heart Fire. Feel your fingers extending further away, far away.
3. Remember: Tan Tien and the universe spiraling. Visualize the universe as a battery charger and yourself as the battery. You are connecting to the charger, charging more fire into yourself.
4. Feel your heart soft in the center as you smile down. Feel the warmth of the fire, the love, joy, and happiness of its energy, in the heart.

5. Feel a connection with the unconditional love of the universe as you keep your heart consciousness in your Lower Tan Tien and extend your awareness out to the universe.

ACTIVATE THE HEART FIRE

Stage 5: Sacred Fire (Chi Fire)

1. Bring your hands together in front of your heart. Feel the fire burning in there.
2. Connect the Heart Fire to the Kidney Fire, the Kidney Fire to the Tan Tien Fire, and the Tan Tien Fire to your Heart Fire, connecting them as one triangular Sacred Fire. Feel the Chi circulating through the lines of the Sacred Fire at one thousand revolutions per minute, and then ten thousand, thirty thousand, and sixty thousand revolutions per minute, doubling and tripling the collective power of the fires.

Stage 6: Open the Third Eye

1. Open your hands. Open and dim your eyes. Look to the universe. From the scapulas, extend your hands to the front, palms vertical. Smile and touch the universe. Extend your hands far away, pushing, pushing, pushing.
2. Turn your palms inward, and extend your middle fingers inward toward your third eye.

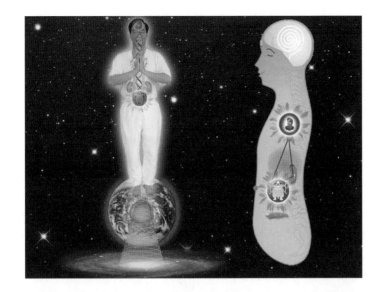

CONNECT THE THREE
FIRES TO CREATE THE
SACRED FIRE

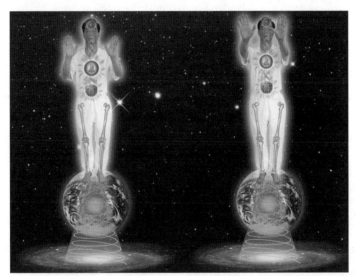

LOOK AS YOU SMILE
INTO THE UNIVERSE
IN FRONT OF YOU

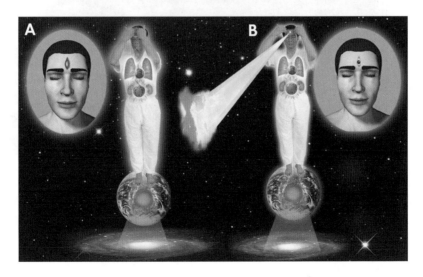

A. THE MIDDLE FINGER HOOKS
INTO THE THIRD EYE.

B. PULL OPEN THE THIRD EYE;
LET HEAVEN OPEN
AND SHINE ITS LIGHT INTO THE
BRAIN.

The Three
Tan Tiens

3. Picture a crack in the middle of your forehead, and pull the crack open. Feel the light from the heavens shining into the brain. Let the light reflect into the organs.
4. Close the third eye.
5. Open and close the third eye three to nine times.

Stage 7: Front Direction Push/Pull Master Practice

1. Push: Turn your palms so that they face away from you. Extend your arms from the scapulas to the front, palms vertical. Feel your hands extend very far away. Expand, smiling and touching the universe—touching the force, touching the Universal Chi.
2. Pull: Moving the arms from the scapulas, draw your hands in a horizontal position toward your body. Draw the Chi back to you from the universe. Think and smile to your Lower Tan Tien.
3. Continue pushing and pulling. When you first start practicing, do at least one hundred repetitions. As you become practiced, increase the repetitions to two hundred.

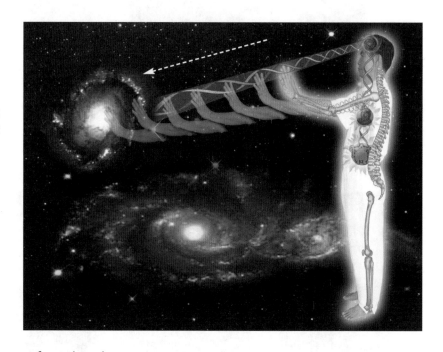

MASTER PRACTICE: TOUCH THE UNIVERSE

Stage 8: Left and Right Directions

1. Move your extended hands from the front horizon to the left and right sides.

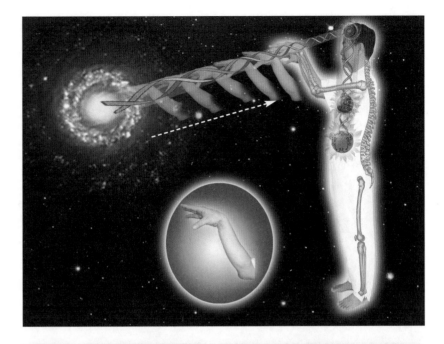

DRAWING UNIVERSAL CHI: FEEL YOUR TAN TIEN AND FILL IT WITH CHI

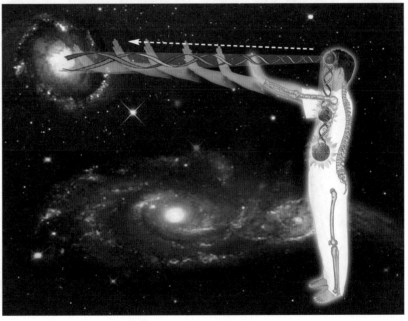

LET GO: PUSH AND TOUCH THE UNIVERSE SIX, NINE, OR EIGHTEEN TIMES

2. Pull the universal energy in. Smile to your Lower Tan Tien. Keep smiling to your Tan Tien.

3. Push to both sides. Expand all the way, smiling and touching the universe.

4. Continue pushing and pulling, touching the universe and drawing the Chi energy into you from both sides, until you have completed 3 to 6 repetitions.

The Three Tan Tiens

TOUCH THE UNIVERSE
TO YOUR LEFT AND TO
YOUR RIGHT

PULL UNIVERSAL
CHI IN. FEEL YOUR
LOWER TAN TIEN.

Stage 9: Direction Above

1. Turn your palms up to the universe. Expand your hands until they are as big as the universe.
2. Turn your body to the left. Scoop up the Universal Chi. Pour the Chi over your crown, and touch your crown. Project the Chi all the way down to the perineum and down through the earth to the universe below. Feel the Chi charge your bones. Always feel your Tan Tien

Tan Tiens

54

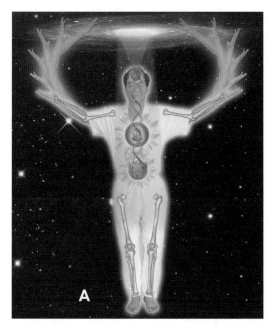 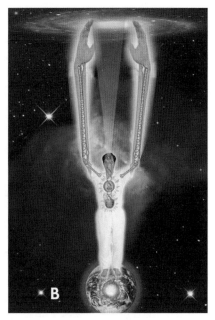

A. Raise your hands above your crown, and feel the crown extend up to heaven. B. Feel that your hands are big and long and that your bones are hollow. Fill and pack the bones with Chi.

Scoop up the Universal Chi and pour it over your head

spiraling, your heart spiraling, your crown spiraling, and the universe around you spiraling.

3. Repeat until you have scooped and gathered the energy three times to the left. Then turn and repeat three times to the right.

Stage 10: Open the Spine

1. Touch the back-crown point. Pour the Chi all over this point. Think of your soles, so that you feel as though a waterfall of Chi flows from your crown all the way down to your soles.

2. Feel your finger grow long and the Chi penetrate down through your spine to the coccyx. Leave the fingers touching the back of the crown to maintain the energetic connection with the coccyx.

3. Focus on the three minds as one, and expand the awareness to the universe. Let yourself be charged by the universe.

4. Maintain awareness of the Tan Tien, and spiral it like universal energy in motion. Feel the heart center spiraling and the crown spiraling. Be aware of the universe spiraling above, below, in front, in back, to the left, and to the right. Let all the sick energy and the negative forces of the body leave and go down into the ground for Mother Earth to recycle. Extend the Chi from above all the way down through the earth and the universe below.

Stage 11: Open the Middle Channel and Perineum

1. Move your hands to the midcrown point. Project your fingers inward; go deeper and deeper through the middle of your body, down to the

FEEL YOUR FINGERS GROWING LONG, ALL THE WAY DOWN TO THE COCCYX

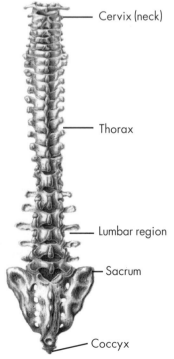

Cervix (neck)

Thorax

Lumbar region

Sacrum

Coccyx

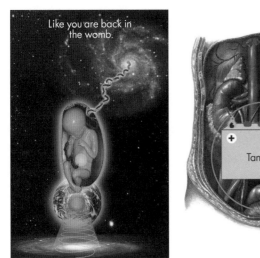

Like you are back in the womb.

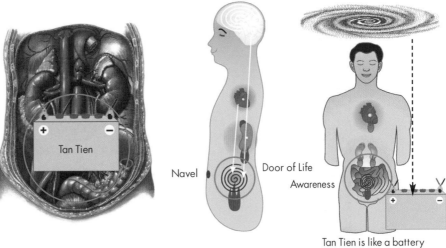

Tan Tien

Navel

Door of Life

Awareness

Tan Tien is like a battery

AS IF YOU WERE BACK IN THE WOMB, YOU PULL DOWN UNIVERSAL CHI
THROUGH THE UMBILICAL CORD OF YOUR CONNECTION TO THE UNIVERSE

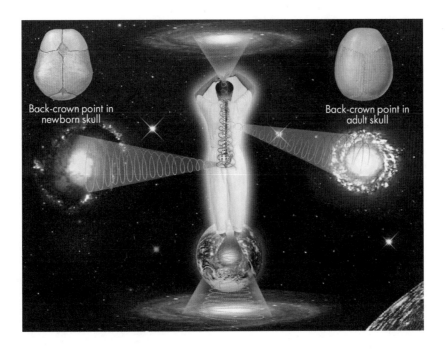

Back-crown point in newborn skull

Back-crown point in adult skull

BE AWARE OF THE LOWER TAN TIEN, THE HEART CENTER, AND THE CROWN SPIRALING. FEEL THE UNIVERSE SPIRALING AND CHARGING THE THREE TAN TIENS.

perineum. Focus on the perineum. Feel the Chi from the universe flow into your perineum.

2. Look for one dot of light. Look into the darkness, the vast darkness, the immense darkness; this is the primordial force, a cloudy moving force. Look for a dot of light at the perineum and extend your awareness all the way down through the ground and the universe below.

The Three
Tan Tiens

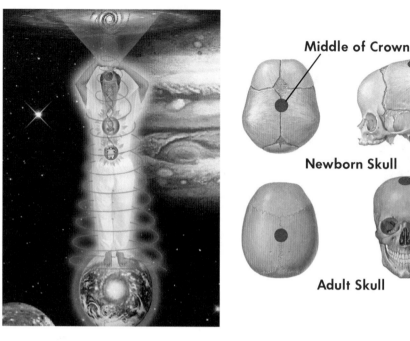

Middle of Crown

Newborn Skull

Adult Skull

MOVE THE HANDS
TO THE MIDDLE OF
THE CROWN AND
FEEL THE FINGERS
PENETRATE TO
THE PERINEUM

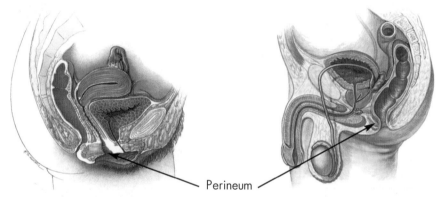

Perineum

Stage 12: Finish

When you are finished opening to the Six Directions and igniting the Three Fires, gather the Chi in your center and bring this expanded awareness into the healing session. Visualize this Chi as an expanding light of knowledge that radiates into the energy field of you and the person you are treating. The universe will do what needs to be done with this intelligence.

OPENING THE THREE TAN TIENS

The Basic Process

Opening the Three Tan Tiens allows you to use your Yi, the three-mind power, repeatedly to recharge your Chi for various purposes. You recharge by connecting to the Universal Chi in the Six Directions simultaneously. In this exercise, the expression "Tan Tien and the universe spiraling" is a reminder to feel your Tan Tien, heart, mideyebrow, and crown spiraling and to feel that you are connected to the universe spiraling in the six directions around you. The basic process of opening a Tan Tien involves four steps.

1. Establish a Location for Chi Entry

To charge a particular area or direct Chi into the body to a particular point, you first must establish a connection point for the Chi by placing a hand or your fingers at an appropriate location on the surface. This gives a location for the Chi to go to. Leave your hand or fingers there even when the Chi starts to go there.

Then move your attention to where you want the Chi to go in the body. Feel the Chi connected to and charging the intended location.

2. Charge Tan Tien from Universe

When the location connection is established, bring your awareness to your spiraling Lower Tan Tien, heart center, mideyebrow, and crown. Be sure that the conscious mind of the heart is lowered to the Lower Tan Tien and the feeling and awareness mind of the abdomen is connected to the mideyebrow and crown and out to the universe. Feel them connected to the spiraling energy in the six directions of the universe. Let the universe charge your Tan Tien.

3. Move Chi to Location

With your focus in the Tan Tien, the Chi will move from there to the location indicated by your hand or fingers and then to the intended destination in the body.

4. Direct Chi Out the Opposite Side to Universe

Don't let the Chi stop in the body, however. Direct your attention to guide the Chi flow through the body and out the opposite side. This will clear any blockages and prevent others from accumulating. It will also release sick energy and negative forces from the body down into the earth. Let the Universal Chi flow out through the universe and beyond.

Having activated the Six Directions and the Three Fires, you are now ready to open the Three Tan Tiens, starting with the Upper Tan Tien.

Upper Tan Tien: Mideyebrow

1. Raise your hands and recharge. Remember: Tan Tien and the universe spiraling.

RAISE YOUR HANDS
AND CHARGE WITH
UNIVERSAL CHI

2. Bring your hands down and touch the mideyebrow. Feel your fingers grow very long and penetrate all the way back to the base of the skull. Focus on the back. Remember: Tan Tien and the universe spiraling. With the spiraling, the Chi in the fingers will become hot. It will expand and penetrate out through the back of the head all the way to the universe behind.

YOUR FINGERS TOUCH
THE MIDEYEBROW
AND PENETRATE TO
THE BACK OF THE
SKULL AND THE
UNIVERSE BEHIND

The Three
Tan Tiens

REMEMBER: TAN TIEN
AND THE UNIVERSE
SPIRALING

3. Picture your fingers as laser beams of Chi. Feel your Tan Tien and the
   universe spiral and charge your fingers. Move your fingers out from
   the mideyebrow around the side of the head to the top of the ears. Your
   fingers are like lasers, cutting open your skull right in the middle and
   around to the top of the ear, cutting open your Upper Tan Tien. Cut
   and project your long fingers into the middle of your brain. Leave your
   fingers there. Concentrate on the spiraling of your Tan Tien, your
   heart, your crown, the universe above, below, front, back, left, and right.
   Your Tan Tien is a big empty space, a primordial force, darkness. You
   can put so much Chi inside there! The Chi penetrates your brain.

MOVE YOUR FINGERS
TO THE TOP OF THE
EARS. FEEL THEM
GROWING LONGER
AND CUTTING OPEN
THE SKULL,
PENETRATING THE
BRAIN.

The Three
Tan Tiens

4. Move your hands all the way to the back, cutting to the back of the skull. Touch, and feel the Upper Tan Tien open.

5. Touch the base of your skull. Focus on the mideyebrow. Feel the Chi flow like a laser beam from back to front and out to the universe in front. Complete the opening process by moving your hands back around to the mideyebrow, cutting as you go.

6. Recharge in the universe. Feel that your bones and your arms are hollow. Fill and compact them with Chi.

7. Scoop up the Universal Chi. Pour it down over your crown and all the way down to the Middle Tan Tien.

RECHARGE IN THE UNIVERSE; SCOOP UP AND POUR THE CHI DOWN TO THE MIDDLE TAN TIEN

The Three
Tan Tiens

Middle Tan Tien: Sternum

1. Bring your hands down to your heart center at the midsternum. Touch. Focus on the point of the spine opposite the heart (between vertebrae T5 and T6). Feel your fingers grow very long. Universal Chi, as a golden light, penetrates your thymus gland. Feel the Chi penetrate through your heart all the way through your spine to the universe behind. Remember: Tan Tien and the universe spiraling. Feel the Chi in your Fingers penetrate into the bone and bone marrow and spread out into your rib cage.

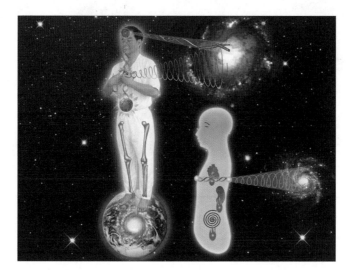

GOLDEN LIGHT ENTERS THE HEART, THYMUS, BONES, AND MARROW; FEEL IT PENETRATE TO THE UNIVERSE BEHIND

2. Raise your hands and recharge. Pour Universal Chi over the crown down through the body, and lower your hands to the heart center. Touch the heart center with your fingertips.

3. Move your hands around under your armpits, extending the Chi like laser beams to cut open the Middle Tan Tien. Pause under the armpits as you send the Chi into your center.

CUT OPEN THE MIDDLE TAN TIEN BY CUTTING AROUND THE ARMPITS

The Three
Tan Tiens

4. Continue to move your hands around to your back until you reach the space between T5 and T6. Touch your fingertips to your spine here and send the Chi from back to front. Let the beam of Chi penetrate out through the heart center to the universe in front of you. Then bring your hands back around the sides to the front, cutting as you go.

Lower Tan Tien: Navel

1. Raise your hands and recharge with Universal Chi. Remember: Tan Tien and Universe spiraling. Your hands are very big and long. The bones are hollow and compacted with compressed Universal Chi. Scoop the Chi from above, pour it over your crown, and guide it down to the navel.
2. Bring your hands to your navel. Touch the navel, and focus on the Door of Life opposite on the spine between the vertebrae L2 and L3. Touch and feel the Chi penetrate to the Door of Life. Remember: Tan Tien and universe spiraling. Feel the Chi penetrate through to the back and out to the universe behind.
3. Charge more Chi into your hands, and let them be like lasers. Use your Chi fingers to cut around to the sides of your body. Pause. The fingers of the left and right hands are very long, extended energetically inside.

A. Recharge the Lower Tan Tien; feel the Chi penetrate through to the Door of Life.
B. Raise your hands to the universe and charge with Chi.
Bring the power down to the Lower Tan Tien.

Cut open the Lower Tan Tien with Chi fingers

Cut and feel the energy penetrate the center. Focus on the Lower Tan Tien and the universe and feel more Chi.

4. Continue cutting to the Door of Life. Touch, and send the Chi from the Door of Life back to the navel and out to the universe in front.

The Three Tan Tiens

CUT OPEN THE DOOR
OF LIFE AND SEND CHI
TO THE NAVEL AND THE
UNIVERSE
IN FRONT

5. Bring your hands back around the sides to the navel, extending the fingers and "cutting" the Tan Tien open as you go. Touch the navel. Remember: Tan Tien and the universe spiraling. Feel more Chi, and feel the Lower Tan Tien open.

Activate Chi in the Bones of Hips, Legs and Sacrum

1. Now touch your pelvic bone by energetically extending your fingers from the front area near the hips to the back. Feel Chi penetrate into your pelvic bones; feel the funny, laughing, happy vibration in the bones.

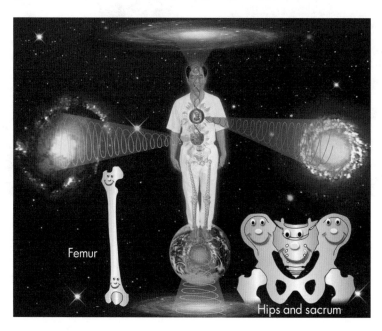

TOUCH THE FEMURS:
HAPPY, LAUGHING
BONES

Femur

Hips and sacrum

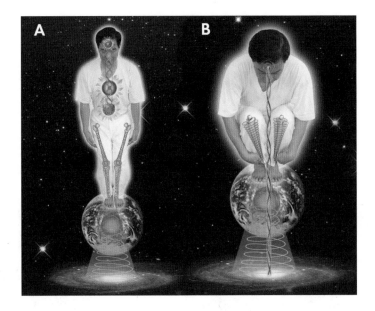

A. SINK THE CHI INTO THE EARTH. B. LOWER AND SINK THE MIND AND CHI DOWN TO THE UNIVERSE.

2. Touch the femur bones. Charge the fingers. Feel the funny, happy, laughing vibration inside the bones and in the bone marrow. Remember: Tan Tien and the universe spiraling. Charge your hands and your bones.

3. Slowly lower the sensation of Chi down through the bones. Move your hands down your legs as you bend. Lower yourself all the way down to the ground, and sit on your feet. Move the Chi with your hands down to your toes, through the earth, and through the universe below.

4. Raise your sacrum, keeping your hands at your toes. Smile to your Lower Tan Tien and feel the Chi from the universe coming to fill the Three Tan Tiens and opening up the sacrum.

RAISE THE SACRUM AND SMILE TO THE TAN TIEN

The Three
Tan Tiens

5. Lower yourself again. Lower the Chi down to the earth and the galaxy below.

6. Once more, raise your sacrum, maintaining hand contact with your feet. Smile to your Tan Tien.

7. For the third time, lower yourself. Open your palms, gathering the Chi from the earth below. Gather and scoop the Chi.

8. Touch your heels and feel your bones as you slowly rise. Fill your bones with Chi as you guide it up your body with your hands.

GATHER THE EARTH CHI

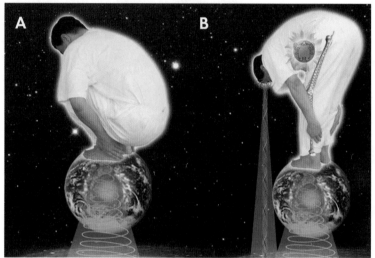

A. FILL THE BONES WITH CHI. B. FEEL YOUR FINGERS PENETRATE THE BONES AS YOU RISE.

9. Fill the bones in the upper legs with Chi as you move your hands up.

10. Feel your bones, and fill them with Chi all the way up to your coccyx. Touch your coccyx. Leave your fingers there. Be aware of the Chi. Feel the Chi rising to the Tan Tien and the universe. Feel it charge the fingers and the spine.

11. Bring your fingers up to the sacrum. Feel the sacrum open. Focus on the Tan Tien and the universe.

12. Bring your hands up to the Door of Life and then back to the navel. You may sit down to continue the next step in whatever Cosmic Healing practice you are undertaking.

Practice daily until you feel the Chi. Then you can apply this Chi to the Healing Sessions.

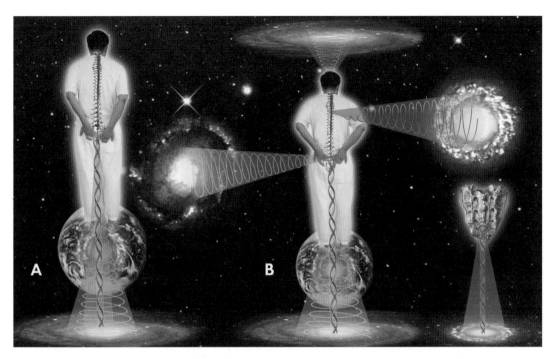

A. Bring Chi to the coccyx. B. Move your hands up to the sacrum, and feel the Chi rise up to the crown.

Bring the Chi to the Door of Life and let it penetrate to the navel

3

Advanced Chi Techniques
Learning to Use Different Types of Chi

CHI SOURCES

There are different sources of Chi in the universe: heavenly, cosmic, earth, and nature. These different sources each provide Chi of a certain color. The different parts of the human body have different energies and, depending on their state of health, respond best to certain colors and color combinations of Chi. Although it is important to learn all the proper applications of the different types of Chi for the different parts of the body, it is more important simply to begin practicing Cosmic Healing Chi Kung, maintaining a serene state of mind throughout. You will immediately realize that Cosmic Healing provides the practitioner with as much benefit as the one being healed. The more you practice, the more you heal.

Universal Chi (Heaven Chi)

Universal Chi, also known as Heaven Chi, includes the energies of all planets, stars, and galaxies and the presence of Universal Love.

Solar Chi is a unique form of heavenly Chi that has different properties at different times of day. Before sunrise or sunset the air contains more white Solar Chi, which we can use abundantly for health and healing. White Chi affects the lungs and the large intestine, so we direct this Chi to these organs. This will generate further Chi to maintain our daily activities.

At midday or midsunset, the air contains more orange or red Solar Chi, which is very powerful.

To practice gathering Solar Chi, look at the horizon at sunrise and sunset. Stand still and extend your palms toward the sun. Smile and absorb the rising or setting sun's energy into yourself.

Cosmic Chi (Air Chi or Man Chi)

Cosmic Chi is the Chi of the higher self. It is named such because Taoists believe that human flesh is formed from the fallen cosmic dust of the universe. Cosmic Chi is in the air around us and nourishes our mind, body, and senses within this physical dimension.

Earth Chi

Earth Chi penetrates the earth and extends several inches above it. It is denser or more closely packed than Cosmic Chi. We can see Earth Chi easily by staring at the horizon for a few minutes at sunset. The "line" that hovers just above the horizon marks the edge of Earth Chi, where the density and movement of Earth Chi interact with that of Cosmic Chi. With practice, you may learn to see Earth Chi just a few inches away, above the ground.

Earth Chi contains yellow and some white Chi. When Earth and Cosmic Chi combine, they become white Chi. This Chi has a very powerful healing energy; it is not overheated but balanced and mild.

Nature Chi and the Five Elements

In Cosmic Healing Chi Kung, we call on the energy of many natural sources, two of which are Earth and Cosmic Chi, to facilitate specific ends. We utilize the color and the unique life force of these forces for different outcomes. Other natural sources include, but are not limited to, the things we can see on the earth: the mountains, lakes, seas, forests, streams, caves, valleys, rocks, and precious stones.

Taoism identifies five elemental forces: earth, metal, water, wood, and fire. The Five Elements, as they're known, can be found in the human body (they correlate to specific organs), in nature, in the air, and in the universe. When we can make a connection to and control our body's elements, we will be able to make connections quickly to nature and the universal forces and employ them easily.

THE HEALING COLORS[*]

White Chi

White Chi is composed of red, orange, yellow, violet, and blue, carrying mild elements of each color. White Chi can be blended with other colors to act as a calming agent for the energy of other colors. It also redirects surplus Chi to areas of the body that need it.

In healing we always use white Chi to add to and tone down other colors that are too powerful, overactive, or hot, so the body can absorb Chi color more easily. We usually use 70 percent white and 30 percent of the other color.

When directing Chi for healing, begin by concentrating shining white Chi at the center of the afflicted area, while directing colored Chi to the edge. If the area needs stronger healing effort, this can also be reversed.

White Chi is safe to use when you are not sure which color might be suitable and especially when you are treating infants, toddlers, the elderly, or the weak.

Blue Chi

The effect of blue Chi is one of cooling and hindering, similar to that of yin or water energy. Its effect is opposite that of red Chi.

Some people's bodies can't adjust immediately to the energy we draw down for healing. In these cases, using blue Chi is helpful because, like the element water, with which it is associated, blue Chi brings harmony and does not cause harm.

Because of blue Chi's ability to cool, soothe, and numb, it is particularly appropriate for promoting relaxation and sleep, reducing abnormally high body temperature, and minimizing pain and swelling. It can also hinder the proliferation of viruses and bacteria and assist in the rapid clotting of blood. Both blue and green Chi can detoxify and energize.

Green Chi

Green Chi is gentle and safe. It can be used to decongest a damaged area by "loosening" it. Once the area has been loosened, you can then use blue Chi

---

*The author has drawn from the ancient teachings of the Indian Vedas, the Taoist masters, and the pioneering work of Darius Dinshah in *Let There Be Light* and Master Choa Kok Sui in *Advanced Pranic Healing* in furthering the science of color healing.

or the color of Chi to which the area is linked in order to expel the disease or damage completely. Green Chi can remove the disease and bad energy by locally sweeping to and then out of either the arms for the upper body or the legs for the lower body.

If an organ needs to be energized with the color of Chi to which it is linked, first energize it with pale green Chi. And always use green Chi before using the violet, orange, or red Chi.

Use the throat to activate and draw green Chi up to the crown, rising to the universe to be multiplied and brought back down for use. When using green Chi in cases where pain is present, always add blue Chi. The motion of pushing and pulling through the affected part is a very powerful healing technique. In a small area or for treating infection, instead of pushing and pulling you can use the "sword fingers" (the middle and index fingers).

Pale green and pale orange Chi can be employed in sequence. The first acts on the "sick" energy, reducing it to a form that can easily be driven out by the second.

Simultaneous use of pale green, pale orange, and white Chi in the ratio 2:1:7 is recommended for treating stubborn ailments, because in this proportion the effect of the group is more intense than that of the sum of its parts.

In the treatment of cancer, employ first blue Chi and then dark green and orange Chi. These colors can assist in toxin removal and in the cleaning and freeing up of disease-affected areas so that necrotic cellular tissue is released. These colors can also relieve congestion and free up "sick" energy that is "stuck"; use them with brushing movements over the affected area. In addition, they help with the treatment of colds and elevated body temperatures and in the dispersal of blood clots.

Red Chi

Light red Chi makes the area to which it is applied stronger, while dark red Chi has the opposite effect. When using color for healing, concentrate shining white in the center and direct light red to the edges for a strengthening effect. Always combine red with blue, green, or white Chi; never use it on its own.

Light red Chi produces qualities of warmth and expansion. When mixed with white, it can help widen blood vessels and breathing tubes. It is good for the circulatory and respiratory systems and is useful for those with heart and asthma problems. It also brings increased energy into the blood and helps allay feelings of fatigue or weakness, driving out "sick" energy along with toxic substances and other waste materials. It can also help those who are sensitive to allergens. For those whose lives are near the end, light red Chi may help prolong life and promote revival of consciousness.

If a person is suffering from a sexually transmitted disease, it is not advisable to treat him or her with crimson Chi. Chi of this color makes the microbes that cause such diseases multiply at a fast rate and can also produce an inflammatory or constrictive reaction.

Orange Chi

Orange Chi should be used only as a pale color that has been diluted with white Chi. Always use blue Chi before using orange Chi. Blue Chi tones down and calms the ailing body area, which is necessary before you can apply the vitality of orange.

Because of its power, orange Chi is inappropriate for treating certain areas. Do not use it with the eyes, heart, head, throat, brain, or spleen. Do not use orange Chi to treat appendix problems, because it could exacerbate the problem.

The large intestine benefits from the use of orange Chi, but this color should be used sparingly on the solar plexus and navel. Orange Chi has a healing effect on the bowel and can also aid in returning an unconscious person to consciousness or in stimulating someone who is dying.

As was mentioned earlier, dark orange Chi can be used together with dark green Chi to treat cancers of certain types.

Orange Chi can also be used to:

> Remove waste products, toxic substances, "sick" energy,
>   viruses, and bacteria
> Relieve menstrual difficulties
> Resolve waste elimination problems
> Free up "sick" energy
> Break down clots in the blood
> Treat problems of the urinary and respiratory systems
> Address diseases of joints and connective tissue
> Banish the common cold
> Relieve problems caused by allergens
> Dissolve cysts

Yellow Chi

Yellow Chi has a close connection to the nerves, the bones, and the bone marrow. It is the color of the spleen, which in Taoism is believed to be involved in the assimilation and processing of food and the appetite. When the spleen is balanced, the appetite will be controlled.

Yellow Chi is beneficial in the treatment of nerves because it promotes nerve regrowth. It helps in the repair of fractures and the cells of bones and connective tissue. It also has the power to increase bone marrow production. It supports the health of bones, tissues, and organs.

Violet Chi

The properties of all the other colors are contained in violet Chi. Therefore, it is particularly effective for treating serious illnesses. Although white Chi also contains the attributes of all the Chi colors, violet Chi infiltrates more readily and to a greater degree than white.

Violet Chi is available in two forms: ordinary violet and electric violet. Ordinary violet Chi comes from the Chi that surrounds us: the air, earth, and sun. Electric violet Chi, on the other hand, is derived from the soul through the crown of the head, the point connected to the North Star and Big Dipper. It is many times more powerful than ordinary violet Chi. The ability to harness electric violet Chi corresponds with the practitioner's level of advancement in developing the crown and higher senses. Because electric violet Chi has been acted upon by the soul, it has the capacity for independent thought and action.

According to Taoist belief, the cup of the Big Dipper gathers all the violet Chi of the universe. To access that violet Chi, the practitioner must reach up to the Big Dipper, grasp its handle with the left hand, and turn the dipper to pour its contents down over the crown. The violet Chi then flows down through the body.

Violet Chi used in combination with other colors intensifies those colors' qualities. If used together with red, orange, green, or yellow Chi, violet Chi can be dangerous; it may cause the undesirable proliferation of some cells. Dark purple Chi should be avoided when diseases of the respiratory system are present, as it could cause the proliferation of disease-causing microbes. In addition, do not use any dark colors with electric violet Chi (either preceding or following its use), as this will produce a very damaging result.

Mauve (light purple) Chi that contains elements of blue and green helps restore organs and nerves affected by disease or trauma. Mauve mixed with white Chi can be used to make a weak area become stronger, but for really fast strengthening a practitioner would use light red Chi mixed with white.

Violet Chi is used to energize an area after pale white/green or pale white/orange is used on an afflicted area, especially the bones. With a brushing movement apply lighter cleansing colors to the whole spinal area and especially to the area where the trauma is located. Then use violet to energize as a last step.

Electric violet Chi can help in the restoration of nerves and organs that have been affected by disease or trauma. It can be used to remove infection and to promote fast healing, even in the case of serious illness.

Dark electric violet has the ability to destroy and can be used for shrinking tumors or suppressing the growth of cancers. However, beforehand, the affected area should be treated with pale blue or green Chi.

As a general guideline, use blue before electric violet.

Gold Chi

Gold Chi, which has almost the same qualities as electric violet Chi, is formed when electric violet Chi meets the spirit body. The color changes to light red when this Chi enters the physical body. However, gold Chi does not have as much influence as the electric violet Chi, being gentler and therefore less effective as a cleansing agent. Gold Chi should be used to treat a very local area, while electric violet Chi can be employed over a wider area.

PERSONAL STARS

Being able to sense and connect with your Personal Stars is necessary in order to connect to the Chi of the universe and the planets. At the moment of conception, yin and yang forces connect with such a force that, only fractions of a second later, they explode, forming nine different energy centers (the chakras). Seven are found in the body. Two are found outside the body, and they form our Personal Stars.

One star is positioned about six inches above the crown; the other is located about three feet below the soles of the feet. As energy centers, the two Personal Stars connect our aural field with the universal and earthly forces.

To connect to your Personal Stars in order to connect to universal and earthly forces, first spiral the three minds into one. Make sure your Lower

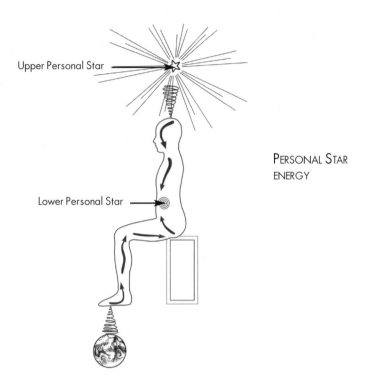

Upper Personal Star

PERSONAL STAR
ENERGY

Lower Personal Star

Tan Tien is warm and the sacrum, mideyebrow, and crown are breathing. See a star or small sun just above your crown. Feel a light beam extend from the crown and make a connection to the star above you. Keep on breathing until you feel a strong connection. Feel how the star above you is exercising a strong pulling force on your crown. Once you feel this pull on your crown, you will also feel a strong pulling force from the earth below your feet. Be aware of the star above you and the earth and universal force below you. Feel that both have a strong pull on you.

Once you have established this strong connection, you may move on to the next part of whichever exercise you are practicing.

PLANETARY CHI

In Taoism, each planet is said to correspond to a particular color, which enhances the planetary force's Chi. Keeping figure 5.1 in front of you, look at the relevant planet and close your eyes. Hold the planet in your mind.

Focus your awareness on the planet above you. Turn your eyes up and look up to your crown. Hold the image of the planet in your mind and extend your sight beyond the crown, looking up into infinity. See the colored light of the planet, and gradually bring it down to your head, until it is about six

Mars—Red Chi Jupiter—Green Chi Venus—White Chi Moon—Silver Chi

Saturn—Yellow Chi Mercury—Blue Chi Sun—Gold Chi Earth—Yellow Chi

THE PLANETS AND THE CORRESPONDING CHI COLORS

feet above you. Form the light into a ball, a holographic image of the planet shining its colored light above you. Invite the ball of light to flow down to your Personal Star (located just above your crown) and then into your Upper Tan Tien for processing. Let it flow down to the appropriate organs. Practice nine to eighteen times, then rest.

Mars: The light is red and flows down to your heart center and the palms of your hand. It can also be breathed in through the sacrum.

Venus: The light is white and flows down into your lungs.

Saturn: The light is yellow and flows down into your spleen. It can also be absorbed from the earth through the soles of your feet and your perineum.

Mercury: The light is blue and is absorbed through the throat center. It flows down to your kidneys.

Jupiter: The light is green and is absorbed through the throat center. It flows down to your liver.

CHANNELING COLOR:
A PRACTICE HEALING SESSION

This session is one that a practitioner undertakes with a student or students. There are two ways to do this type of healing session. One is to focus on the specific location in your own body, using your hands, and to ask the other person to do the same on his or her own body. Together, you complete the entire route. Another way is to focus on your own energy body and ask the student to do the same. Bring a channel or line down from your energy body into your physical body and do the same for the student. Once again, complete the routes together.

For reasons of clarity, this text mentions only one student and uses the male gender; this session may, however, be performed with a group and, of course, with persons of either gender. Before starting the session, do some group meditation practice and warm-up exercises.

CHANNEL THE
PLANETARY ENERGY
INTO THE BODY WHILE
FOCUSING
ON THE COLORS

Advanced Chi Techniques

1. Be aware of the Lower Tan Tien and connect to the universe. Let the student sit with his back to you. You are standing behind him. Be aware of your sacrum area and feel the Chi; wait for the Chi to rise up to the crown and to the universe. Spiral the Chi down to the student's and your own energy body and it will flow into the physical realm.

2. Draw in the green light with your palm. Push it right through the sacrum and disperse the sickness through to the other side of the universe. Pull the green light from the universe through the sacrum, and push the sick Chi out to the universe. When you pull back, stop the green Chi at the student's sacrum; there is no need to pull it back to you. Keep pushing and pulling until you have completed six to nine cycles and you feel the sacrum has been cleaned.

3. Yellow light from the earth will help strengthen the sacral bone. Draw in the yellow light with your palm. Visualize the sacrum and vitalize the complete bone structure with yellow light passing through it.

4. Be aware of the energy body above the crown. Extend yourself above your crown and channel down the white light from the center of the universe and the violet light from the North Star. Using your mind, ask the bones to open, allowing the white and violet light to flow into the marrow. Focus on the energy body; you can picture the energy body's sacrum and bone structure to help guide the energy inside and see the whole body light up from deep within.

5. Then focus on the Door of Life and the navel. First flush them through with green light, cleaning them out. Draw the green light from the Door of Life through to the navel, and then push back through. To cool down the Door of Life (if necessary), draw the blue light and push it through from the navel to the Door of Life, connecting with the universe. Then bring the white or violet light down and activate the Lower Tan Tien.

6. Concentrate on the solar plexus and the Chi Chung point (at vertebra T11). Once again, draw the green light, spiral it, use it to flush the areas, then energize them with white and violet light. As before, always allow the energy to stream through both the points completely.

The solar plexus holds all the emotions. When working on the solar plexus, the most important thing to remember is to connect the "backside" to the universe. There is literally no end to this connection. Just allow the Chi to come all the way down and then pull it toward the rear slightly. Simply clean out the path. Allow the information to condense; allow any images to manifest and then release. Then stabilize the energy. Picture the Chi field enveloping the person as a big protective bubble. Cool down with blue light.

7. Proceed to the heart and the Shen Dao, a point along the spine between the fifth and sixth thoracic vertebrae (T5 and T6). Draw in and push through the green light; repeat several times. Now scan the heart with your palm, sensing its strength. Select an appropriate hue of red, one that is not too dark. Send the red light through the heart to strengthen it. Use blue light to cool down any excess heat in the heart, flushing down and out. Draw in white Chi, then push it through to the Shen Dao. Energize the center at the back of the heart using violet and gold Chi. Picture the heart surrounded by a golden aura.

8. Move up to the throat center. Flushing through the throat center to the C7 vertebra, using first blue light to open and clear it and then green light to clean.

9. Next activate the mideyebrow. Focus on the mideyebrow in your own body. Use gold-yellow Chi to flush and stabilize the mideyebrow. Flush it all the way through to the backside of the head. Energize with violet-gold light.

10. Proceed up to the third eye in the middle of the forehead. Connect to the Kun Lun point (at the back of the crown). Flush through both points using the pale violet light. Energize with intense white or gold light.

11. Concentrate on the crown. Use violet or gold light to enter and flush all the way down through the Central Channel (the center channel of the Thrusting Channel; see page 90), leaving the body at the perineum. Cool down the system by showering blue light over the whole body.

THE SPLEEN AND SOLAR PLEXUS: CHI DELIVERY ROUTES

The spleen and solar plexus are connected to each other and the navel, the major center that connects to all the organs. The navel, in turn, is connected to the Door of Life; they sit opposite each other. We call this an emotional link.

When you are working with Chi, it is vitally important to maintain and support the health of the spleen and solar plexus. White Chi is taken in mainly at the spleen, where it is split into its colored forms of red, green, purple, blue, and orange and sent to the various parts of the body. If the solar plexus becomes clogged up, the spleen will also become blocked, and vice versa. All the energy of the body would eventually become stuck at this main juncture.

Buddha Palm
The Cosmic Healing Training Form

THE BUDDHA PALM

Cosmic Healing Chi Kung is also known as Buddha Palm or the Empty Force sequence. For the sake of this text, we will refer to the training form as Buddha Palm. The term "form" means a series of movements. Buddha Palm as a training form looks a lot like Tai Chi (moving Chi Kung). Each movement in the Buddha Palm form is designed to train the practitioner in the movement and channeling of Chi.

The Buddha Palm is composed of four sections:

Section I: Connect to Heaven and Earth
Section II: Open the Bridge and Regulator Channels
Section III: Open the Functional, Governor, and Thrusting
    Channels
Section IV: Activate One-Finger Art and the Chi Belt

These sections teach you how to project Chi through the space in the cosmos, through the space between your hands, and through space to others. When a Cosmic Healing Chi Kung practitioner touches another, he or she usually picks up "sick" energy from that person. This practice will teach you how to ground the sick energy to the earth and to disperse it into the universe to be decomposed and recycled by the planets.

The Buddha Palm's other name, Empty Force, refers to the concept of strength without muscle, of force as a result of kinetic ability and achievement through strength of will and energetic control. It is the ultimate balance. When we say "be tense without tensing," we refer to squeezing tendon or muscle against bone while still maintaining agility and flexibility, thus being iron on the inside and soft as cotton on the outside. This concept is easier to feel than to intellectualize. Just know that as you master this principle, it will become self-evident.

Practice the Buddha Palm until you can project Chi from your palms and fingers and feel Chi coming into your body through your hands. The most important part of this practice is always to remain connected with the universal force coming from the Six Directions. If you focus on healing from your hands or your Tan Tien, you will use up your own energy. You must be connected to Universal Chi.

Learn to expand your awareness to nature, the oceans, the lakes, the forests, and the mountains. Smile to nature, and feel it smile back to you; inhale and draw the Chi into your palms. Expand your awareness to connect to the light, the Milky Way, and the cosmos.

Be aware of the heart and the red light in the heart; expand your awareness to infinity. The light will come close to you; picture the red planet Mars above you. See it shine down to your crown, feeling the light in your palms. Be aware of the Six Directions, and feel your body growing bigger until you touch the sky, with your feet still planted in the earth.

THE MERIDIANS OF THE BODY

Sections II, III, and IV involve opening the meridians, or channels of Chi flow, in the body. The channels are divided into two major groups: the extraordinary channels and the ordinary channels. After your mother's egg and your father's sperm joined together to form a single cell, that cell began to divide. The extraordinary channels were the first energy channels formed as a result of that early cell division.

The Eight Extraordinary Channels
Governor Channel
Functional or Conception Channel
Thrusting Channel
Belt Channel
Yang Regulator Channel
Yin Regulator Channel
Yang Bridge Channel
Yin Bridge Channel

Later, as your fetus developed, your Original Chi flowed through the eight extraordinary channels to help create your internal organs and their twelve energy channels. These twelve "ordinary" channels are divided into yin and yang. The yin channels are connected to the solid organs, and the yang channels are connected to the hollow organs.

The Twelve Ordinary Channels

Lung (Yin) Channel

Large Intestine (Yang) Channel

Stomach (Yang) Channel

Spleen (Yin) Channel

Heart (Yin) Channel

Small Intestine (Yang) Channel

Bladder (Yang) Channel

Kidney (Yin) Channel

Pericardium (Yin) Channel

Triple Warmer (Yang) Channel

Gallbladder (Yang) Channel

Liver (Yin) Channel

These twelve organs serve to extract energy from the food and water we ingest and the air that we breathe to create energy through the metabolic processes of respiration, circulation, digestion, elimination, and reproduction. This energy is called Postnatal Chi, because it comes in after we are born. Thus the extraordinary channels serve as the link between our Original or Prenatal Chi, which came from our mother and father, and our Postnatal Chi, which comes from our food and air as a result of metabolism.

General Functions of the Eight Extraordinary Channels

They serve as reservoirs of Chi.

About two thousand years ago, one of the great texts of Chinese medicine, the *Nan Ching*, was written. This classic text describes the twelve ordinary channels as rivers and the eight extraordinary channels as reservoirs of Chi. When the ordinary channels become low in energy, they can draw from the reservoirs of energy in the extraordinary channels. On the other hand, if the ordinary channels become too full, the excess can be taken up by the extraordinary channels. In this way, the extraordinary channels help us maintain balance in our energy body.

They store and circulate Ching Chi.

The extraordinary channels all draw their energy from the kidneys, which are the storehouse of Ching Chi (essence or sexual energy) in the body. Thus the extraordinary channels circulate Ching Chi around the body, particularly to the skin and hair, and to the five ancestral organs: the brain and spinal cord, the bone marrow, the blood, the uterus, and the liver and gallbladder.

They circulate Defensive Chi to protect the body.

The Chi that protects the body against invasion by external pathogens is called Defensive Chi or Wei Chi. The extraordinary channels known as the Governor Channel, the Functional Channel, and the Thrusting Channel circulate Defensive Chi over the back, abdomen, and thorax, respectively.

They regulate our life cycles.

In the first chapter of *Huang Di Nei Ching Su Wen* (The Yellow Emperor's Classic of Internal Medicine), another of the classic texts of Chinese medicine, the life changes of women and men are described as occurring in seven- and eight-year cycles, respectively. The Functional Channel and the Thrusting Channel govern these cycles.

The Eight Extraordinary Channels and Chi Kung

Few texts are available today that describe the purpose and function of the eight extraordinary channels and their place in Chi Kung practice. To make matters more confusing, though they may bear the same name, the meridians and points used in Chi Kung are often quite different from those used in acupuncture. This is because their purposes are different.

Chinese medicine aims to restore sick people to health. The points being treated must be superficial so that they can be activated by acupuncture needles. Chi Kung and Taoist meditation, on the other hand, aim to maintain health and to take one beyond mere physical health to spiritual immortality. The channels and points can be deep within the body, since the energy is guided by the mind or by postures and movements rather than by needles.

Most acupuncturists, with the exception of some modern Japanese researchers, pay little attention to the eight extraordinary channels in diagnosis and treatment. In contrast, the extraordinary channels have been of special importance to Taoists and Chi Kung practitioners for thousands of years. Taoists see the extraordinary channels as the foundation of our bodily energy, as the bridge between our Original or Prenatal Chi and our Postnatal Chi; these channels affect us on the deepest level of our basic constitutional energy.

Therefore, Taoists focus on opening up the flow of energy through the eight extraordinary channels as a prerequisite for opening the energy flow in the twelve ordinary channels. In the Universal Tao system, you open the Governor Channel and the Functional Channel in the Microcosmic Orbit meditation. The second pair, the Thrusting Channel and the Belt Channel, is opened in the second level of the Fusion of the Five Elements meditation. The remaining four channels, the Yin and Yang Bridge Channels and the Yin and Yang Regulator Channels, are opened in the third level of Fusion of the Five Elements. After the eight extraordinary channels are open, in the next level of Taoist inner alchemical meditation called the Lesser Enlightenment of Kan and Li, the twelve ordinary channels are then opened.

Parts II, III, and IV of the Empty Force sequence will teach you to access and activate the eight extraordinary channels. The movements used in this activation are relatively simple. To completely master the eight extraordinary channels, however, you must learn and practice the meditations described above. Once you have done so, the Empty Force practice of Cosmic Healing Chi Kung will be particularly powerful and balancing for you.

SUMMARY: THE BUDDHA PALM SEQUENCE

Each of the four sections of Cosmic Healing Chi Kung develops a different type of energy mastery. Each is composed of opening movements, core movements, and closing movements. Opening movements are designed to connect and prepare the practitioner for practice. They open the practitioner to the work ahead and focus the mind. Core movements are specific training techniques for the specific Chi Kung being practiced. Closing movements signal the mind and body to finish the practice. They tend to be gathering-type movements that collect Chi in the body for storage.

Practice each part daily for one to two weeks, or until you can do it well. Then you can proceed to learning the next part.

Section I: Connect to Heaven and Earth

The first section of Cosmic Healing Chi Kung emphasizes connecting to the Chi emanating from heaven and earth. This ability is very beneficial for self-healing and is essential for healing others. If we do not connect to some source of external energy when healing others, we must draw upon our own personal reservoirs. Our personal Chi is limited by nature and can easily become depleted if we give it away too freely.

Over the past decade, Chi Kung healing has become very popular in

China. There are now hundreds of Chi Kung hospitals and clinics throughout the country. Yet many of the Chi Kung therapists can administer only two or three treatments a day; they spend the rest of their day practicing Chi Kung to replenish their own Chi. Those who practice the more traditional Chi Kung know how to connect to the Chi of heaven and earth.

Cosmic Healing Chi Kung teaches us that nature and its energies are the source of our power. In Taoism, nature and the universe are equivalent to God. You are a part of nature and can easily learn to open to the forces in the macrocosm and let them flow through you. Just tune in to the frequencies around you.

Earth Chi: When you stand or sit, be aware of your soles (the Bubbling Spring points) making a good connection with the earth. Your perineum is relaxed and open. You are connecting to the yin force of the earth and can expand further down to the other side of the universe.

Heaven Chi: When you draw in your chin, slightly relax your chest, and tilt your head slightly forward, you begin to be aware of the yang force of heaven.

Cosmic Chi: The qualities of the Five Elements reveal themselves as woody trees (growing force), fiery deserts (expanding force), earth mountains (stabilizing force), metal air (contracting force), and watery oceans and lakes (gathering force). We call the combination of these elements Cosmic Chi. When you breath in, be aware of the Five Elements in the air. Allow Cosmic Chi to move through your body.

In this first section, you will learn to sense the energies outside your body. You will then learn to draw and absorb these energies into your body and process them in order to use them for healing. This is the essence of Chi Kung. Today, there is a lot of emphasis on learning movements and forms of Chi Kung. However, if the inner feeling is not there, the movements are of little value.

Section II: Open the Bridge and Regulator Channels

In this section, you will learn to open and strengthen four of the Eight Extraordinary Channels: the Yin and Yang Bridge and Regulator Channels. This section also teaches you to extend and take in Universal Chi and emit Chi from the body for healing others. This ability is the heart of Cosmic Healing Chi Kung practice.

The Bridge and Regulator Channels have no points of their own but, instead, "borrow" points from the ordinary channels. They travel along the same paths as the ordinary channels; there is no real difference between them.

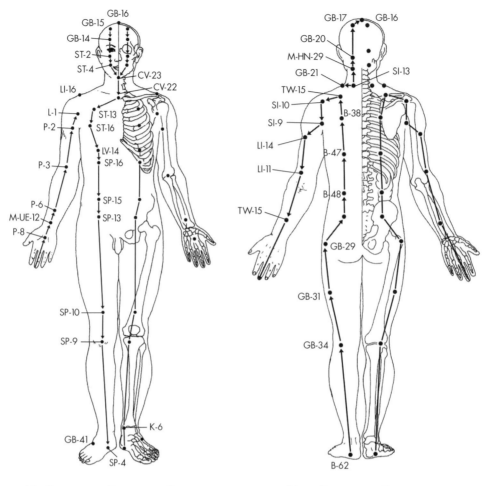

YIN BRIDGE AND REGULATOR CHANNELS

YANG BRIDGE AND REGULATOR CHANNELS

The Bridge and Regulator channels connect or bridge and regulate the flow of Chi through all the body's meridians.

The Yin and Yang Bridge Channels, also called the Heel Vessels because they originate at the heels, regulate the amount of energy being used by all the other meridians in the body. They act like a bridge, linking together the stored Chi in the body and the areas in need of Chi. If any meridian uses more energy than it needs to flow properly, usually other meridians become deficient as a result. The Bridge Channels seek to assure that your energy is distributed in a balanced way. The Yin Bridge Channel runs along the front or yin side of the body, while the Yang Bridge Channel runs along the back or yang side of the body.

The Regulator Channels, also called the Linking Vessels, bind together all the meridians in the body. The Regulator Channels are also divided into yin and yang. The yin aspect, which runs along the front of the body, moves yin energy and regulates the blood and inner parts of the body. It connects with all the yin channels: the Liver, Spleen, Kidney, Heart, Pericardium, and Lung Channels. The yang aspect, which runs along the back side of the body, moves yang energy, controls Defensive Chi, regulates resistance to external infections, and regulates the external parts of the body. It connects with all the yang channels: the Stomach, Bladder, Gallbladder, Large Intestine, Triple Warmer, and Small Intestine Channels. By joining together the various ordinary channels, the Regulator Channels help maintain a harmonious and cooperative interaction among them.

The Regulator Channels in Taoist Yoga and Chi Kung are slightly different from those presented in acupuncture texts. The Chi Kung Regulator Channels include the yin and yang arm routes; some Taoist Yoga texts refer to the arm routes as the Yin Yu and the Yang Yu. Acupuncture texts, in contrast, include only the leg, trunk, and head routes. Many recent Chi Kung texts, unaware of these differences, depict illustrations from acupuncture texts alone, further adding to the confusion.

Disorders of the Bridge Channels

Excess Yang Energy

When yin energy is slowed down in the Bridge Channels, yang energy flows more rapidly. The excess yang can cause insomnia, difficulty in closing the eyes, hypertension, stiff back and waist, inability to bend down, thigh tumors, bad colds, spontaneous sweating, headaches, painful eyes, paralysis of the arms and legs, vomiting of milk in infants, deafness, epilepsy, nose bleeding, swelling of the body, pain in the joints, and head sweating.

Excess Yin Energy

When yang energy is slowed down in the Bridge Channels, yin energy moves more rapidly. The excess yin can cause sleepiness, difficulty in keeping the eyes open, hypotension, choking, painful urination, stomach rumbling, vomiting, diarrhea, difficult bowel movements, difficult labor, and unconsciousness.

Disorders of the Regulator Channels

Excess Yang Energy

When yin energy is slowed down in the Regulator Channels, yang energy moves more rapidly. The excess yang can cause swelling and pain in the joints, cold knees, paralysis of the arms and legs, painful back and sides, aching muscles, fever, rashes, night sweating, tetanus, painful red eyes, colds, superficial fevers, and pain in the head, neck, and edge of the eyebrows.

Excess Yin Energy

When yang energy is slowed down in the Regulator Channels, yin energy moves more rapidly. The excess yin can cause heart pain, diarrhea with stomach rumbling, difficulty swallowing, pain on both sides of the chest, diseases associated with cold, and convulsions.

Section III: Open the Functional, Governor, and Thrusting Channels

The third section teaches you to enhance the energy in the points along the Functional and Governor Channels, the reservoirs of yin and yang energy in the body. The Functional or Conception Channel is yin, and all of the ordinary yin channels connect to it. The Governor Channel is yang, and all of the ordinary yang channels connect to it.

The Functional and Governor Channels are also used in the Microcosmic Orbit. Opening the Microcosmic Orbit strengthens and balances your energy and prepares you to heal others. Practicing this section will be of great help with the Microcosmic Orbit meditation.

The Thrusting Channel may be used to bring energy up from the feet, through the body, and out the head. It has three parts: a red channel on the left side of the body, a silver channel through the middle, and a blue channel on the right. The center channel is also known as the Central Channel. Practitioners of Chi Kung sometimes use it independent of the other channels.

In Section III we also begin to focus more on the sensation of Chi being emitted from our palms during the Chi ball exercise. This energy is emitted primarily from the Laogong points, but you can also feel it throughout the palms and fingers. It will feel like a balloon between your hands that is expanding and contracting or like two magnetic fields repelling and attracting each other.

Once you have practiced Cosmic Chi Kung for a while and have become skillful at it, you may find that grasping the Chi ball is all you need to do to activate your flow of healing energy. As you become sensitive to the sensation of your own Chi, it becomes an easy step to feel the Chi of others.

Section IV: Activate One-Finger Art and the Chi Belt

In this final section of Cosmic Healing Chi Kung, you will focus on opening the yin and yang channels of the arms and on activating the Chi Belt around

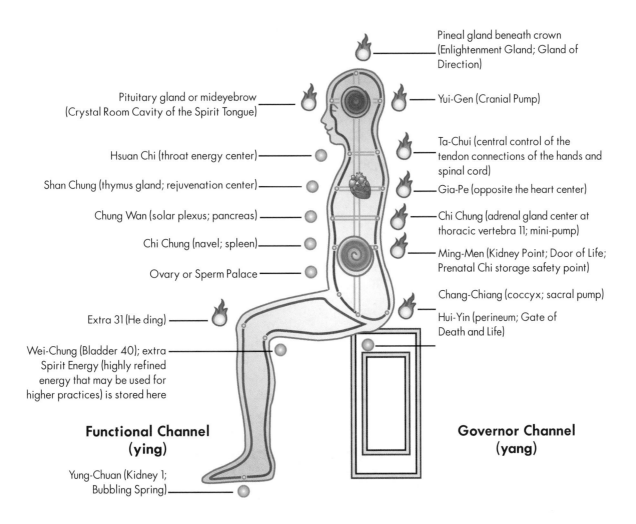

Pineal gland beneath crown (Enlightenment Gland; Gland of Direction)

Yui-Gen (Cranial Pump)

Pituitary gland or mideyebrow (Crystal Room Cavity of the Spirit Tongue)

Ta-Chui (central control of the tendon connections of the hands and spinal cord)

Hsuan Chi (throat energy center)

Gia-Pe (opposite the heart center)

Shan Chung (thymus gland; rejuvenation center)

Chi Chung (adrenal gland center at thoracic vertebra 11; mini-pump)

Chung Wan (solar plexus; pancreas)

Chi Chung (navel; spleen)

Ming-Men (Kidney Point; Door of Life; Prenatal Chi storage safety point)

Ovary or Sperm Palace

Chang-Chiang (coccyx; sacral pump)

Hui-Yin (perineum; Gate of Death and Life)

Extra 31 (He ding)

Wei-Chung (Bladder 40); extra Spirit Energy (highly refined energy that may be used for higher practices) is stored here

Functional Channel (ying)

Governor Channel (yang)

Yung-Chuan (Kidney 1; Bubbling Spring)

THE MICROCOSMIC ORBIT: DEPENDING ON WHETHER IT IS OPEN OR CLOSED, EACH POINT OF THE MICROCOSMIC ORBIT HAS AN EFFECT ON THE BODY

the waist. Mastery of this aspect of Cosmic Healing Chi Kung will enhance your ability to project Chi through your fingers for healing.

Yin and Yang Channels of the Arms

Six important energy channels flow through the arms. Three channels are yin and three are yang. The six channels are paired together, with each pair composed of one yin channel and one yang channel. The yin channel of each pair flows down the inside of the arm from torso to fingertip, while its yang counterpart flows up the outside of the arm from fingertip to head.

The pairs are as follows:

Metal Element	Yin	Lung Channel	Thumb
	Yang	Large Intestine Channel	Index finger
Fire Element	Yin	Pericardium Channel	Middle finger
	Yang	Triple Warmer Channel	Ring finger
Fire Element	Yin	Heart Channel	Pinkie finger
	Yang	Small Intestine	Pinkie finger

Emitting Chi from the fingers for healing is known as the One-Finger Art. Because the energy channels of the arms either end or begin at the fingertips, the fingers are very effective instruments for projecting healing energy. Your fingers can focus energy like a laser beam toward a concentrated area such as a specific acupuncture point. You can also emit energy from all the fingers at once, creating a combined effect to target an area. Section IV of Cosmic Healing Chi Kung will stimulate all of the arm channels and give you an opportunity to activate all of the fingers for beaming energy.

ONE-FINGER ART

The Belt Channel (Dai Mo)

The Belt Channel, also known as the Dai Mo, Chi Belt, or Girdle Vessel, is the only channel in the body that runs horizontally. It encircles the body at the waist level, connecting all the vertical channels that run through the torso. Thus, the Belt Channel plays an important role in maintaining good energetic communication between the upper and lower body. In women, it strongly affects the uterus and the menstrual cycle in particular.

In Taoist Chi Kung, the Belt Channel is not thought to be limited to the waist region but, instead, is said to encircle the entire body, almost like an energetic cocoon woven around you from head to foot. Activating the Belt Channel strengthens your aura and helps defend and protect you from outside negative energies.

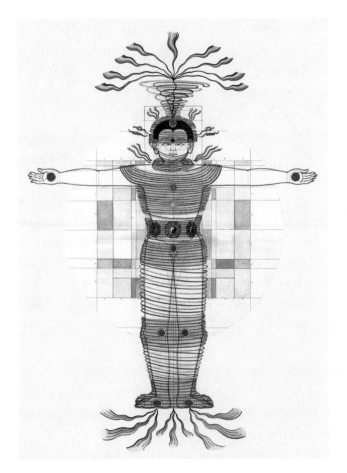

THE BELT CHANNEL

COSMIC HEALING CHI KUNG PREPARATION

Cosmic Chi Kung can be practiced in either a sitting or a standing position.

Sitting: Sit on the edge of a chair, with your feet flat on the ground. Place your hands on your upper legs. Keep your back as straight as possible. Relax.

Standing: Stand with your feet parallel and shoulder width apart. Tilt your sacrum and pelvis slightly forward until you feel your feet press more firmly into the ground. As you tilt the pelvis, feel your lumbar vertebrae pressing outward; this is called "Opening the Door of Life." Relax your chest and sink your sternum. Draw your chin in slightly, and hold your head, neck, and spine erect as if your head and spine were suspended from above by a string.

1. Open a connection with heaven and earth force through the palms, as described on pages 96–97.
2. Create a Chi dome, as described on pages 148–149.
3. Invoke the Cosmic Inner Smile. Be aware of your heart and listen to your kidneys with your inner senses. Smile to your heart and kidneys and feel them pulsing; feel them communicating and interacting with each other. The Kan and the Li—the water of the kidneys and the fire of the heart—balance and begin to mix.
4. Raise your arms slightly, as if you were holding a Ping-Pong ball in each armpit. Slightly move your fingers to activate the Chi flow. Relax. Feel the sensations of the Chi flow: tingling, warmth, pulsing, electric, and magnetic.
5. Be aware of your palms. Draw in Chi by activating the Bone Breathing process. Become aware of the perineum; slightly pull up the perineum, sexual organs, and anus and "connect the bridge," as described on page 99, relaxing the perineum.
6. Breathe into the palms of the hands and the soles of the feet, further enhancing your connection to the earth force. Smile to the blue earth energy as it flows up your arms and legs and suffuses your body with pleasant Yin energy.
7. Breathe into the mideyebrow point and activate your connection with Cosmic Chi. Smile to the golden light of the cosmic energy as it swirls into your mideyebrow point and flows throughout your body, healing and balancing your energy.
8. Breathe into your crown point and activate your connection with the Heaven Chi. Smile to the red and violet light of the heavenly force as it flows into your brain and washes your body with subtle pure Yang energy.
9. Place the tip of your tongue on the upper palate behind the teeth in a comfortable position.
10. As you begin to move through the postures of Cosmic Healing Chi Kung, always be aware of the Chi flow and its attending sensations.

Throughout parts I, II, III, and IV, the phrase "Tan Tien and universe spiraling" serves as a reminder to feel your Tan Tien, heart, mideyebrow, and

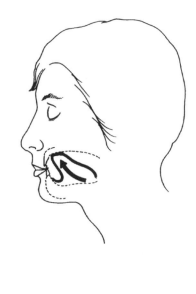

INVOKE THE COSMIC INNER SMILE

PLACE THE TIP OF THE TONGUE ON THE
UPPER PALATE

crown spiraling and to feel that you are connected to the universe spiraling in the six directions around you.

In the four sections that follow, hold each of the Cosmic Healing Chi Kung postures for five to thirty seconds. As you become more experienced, gradually lengthen that time to one to two minutes. While holding the postures, count the breath for five to fifteen seconds, being aware of the Tan Tien and feeling the Chi in the Tan Tien move up to the crown and expand up to the universe; fuse your Chi with the Universal Chi and let it multiply down to your palms. Just concentrate on "Tan Tien and the universe spiraling"; do not concentrate on the palms at all.

Forget about Your Palms

An extremely important principle of Cosmic Healing hand techniques is to "forget about your palms." You should use the palm (which is incredibly sensitive) only for "guiding" the universal energy into the right spot, sending out a minute beam of light, like a laser, that marks the place where the energy should be sent. Your palm is connected to your brain, which has been sunk into your Lower Tan Tien. The light marker will serve as a beacon for the force that is directed down by your mind. Draw down the Universal Chi, guide it to the right spot, and give the command "Stay." The energy is directed by your mind, not your palm. This is very important, because otherwise the Chi will disappear once you move your hand.

Opening Heaven and Earth Force in the Palms

The purpose of this technique is to draw in the forces of heaven and earth through the palm. This is accomplished by using the palms to draw spirals, the symbol of heaven and earth force. As you draw the spirals, you should actually feel the palm breathing, inhaling these forces. In the beginning, however, you may only be able to use your own mental imagery and imagine that you are absorbing these forces. In time, the feelings will replace your imagination.

You breathe in Heaven Chi when you draw the heaven spirals and Earth Chi when you draw the earth spirals. You may draw both in one session; you may also choose to draw in just one if you feel you need more of one or the other. It is important to balance these energies whenever you do this exercise.

1. Begin by raising the right hand to about shoulder height, with the elbow sunk and the palm facing forward. Slightly pull back (open) the index finger, and slightly stretch the thumb forward and down. This will activate the Laogong point on the palm. Bring together the tips of the thumb and index finger on your left hand. This will allow the right hand to draw in Heaven and Earth Chi. The left hand will then be held palm up to draw in Heaven Chi or palm down to draw in Earth Chi.

2. Bring your left hand to your side, holding it palm up with thumb and index tips touching each other. With your right hand, begin drawing the heaven spiral by moving the palm in a clockwise motion, with the circles getting smaller and smaller, spiraling inward. Draw seven or nine (corresponding to the number of planets in our solar system) small spirals, drawing in the violet heavenly energy.

3. Lower your right hand slightly and turn your left palm down to face the earth. With your right hand, begin drawing the earth spiral, moving the palm in a counterclockwise motion, with the circles getting larger and larger. Draw five (the number of elements) spirals, drawing in the blue earth energy as you move. Inhale into the palm, feeling the energies.

4. You may now bring both hands down to the beginning position of Cosmic Healing Chi Kung, or you may open the Cosmic Channel to

the planets for healing, as is discussed in "Part I: Opening to Heaven and Earth."

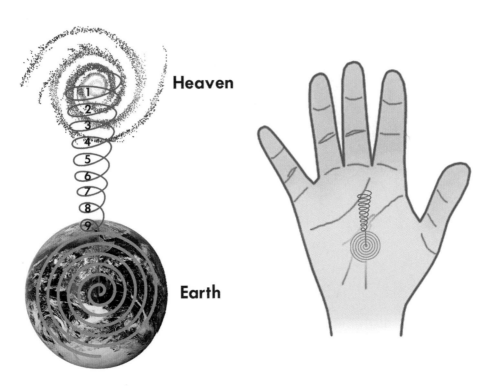

THE SPIRAL MOVEMENT TRACES THE SYMBOL OF HEAVEN AND EARTH CHI IN THE LAOGONG POINT (PERICARDIUM 8)

Connecting the Bridge

Contracting the muscles of the perineum, sexual organs, and anus activates our connection with the earth energy. By pulling up these areas and drawing in energy through the soles of the feet, you immediately become grounded and bring the earth (yin) energy into the Microcosmic Orbit. Pulling up should be done gently and directed by the Yi.

When we speak of "connecting the bridge," we are referring to the above exercise, except that after the first contraction you relax the perineum. Following on the principles of a siphon, when you then relax the perineum, the earth energy will continue to flow into the body. You thus connect the "bridge" across the perineum from the sexual organs to the anus, using the Yi to direct the energy. This actively combines the earth energy and your sexual energy and directs it into the Microcosmic Orbit. This energy is circulated during Cosmic Healing Chi Kung. Holding a very gentle contraction will keep you grounded during the exercise. It can be done sitting or standing.

Buddha
Palm

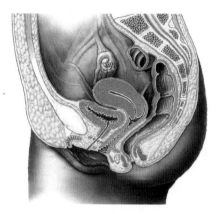

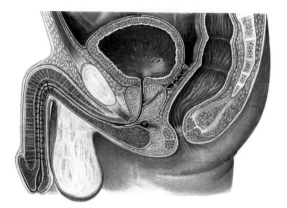

WOMEN LIGHTLY CONTRACT THE VAGINA

MEN LIGHTLY CONTRACT THE ANUS, PERINEUM, AND SEXUAL ORGANS

CONNECTING THE BRIDGE COMBINES EARTH AND HEAVEN CHI

BUDDHA PALM OPENING MOVEMENTS

The four sections of the Empty Force sequence are each practiced in three parts: opening movements, core movements, and closing movements. The opening and closing movements for each section are the same. To undertake a section, practice the opening movements described here, then the core movements of that particular section, and finally the closing movements described at the end of this chapter.

Three Minds into One Mind

1. Empty the mind and heart down to the Lower Tan Tien. (See the description of this exercise on page 64.)
2. Hold the hands together at the heart center. Smile and make the heart feel soft; feel love, joy, and happiness. Turn your consciousness inward and your awareness out.
3. Feel your legs lengthen, extending down to the center of the earth. Feel your hands lengthen, extending to the universe below. Let your mind expand, and be aware all the way down to the universe.
4. Feel the bones of the arms and legs, and begin bone breathing. Feel Universal Chi filling, packing, and compressing into the bones.
5. Draw this Chi down to the back of your crown. Feel a heavy pressure on the crown and a slightly numb or light electric downward flow, like oil dripping down. Remember: Tan Tien and universe spiraling. Count to five.

Channeling the Earth Force: Marrow Washing

1. Smile into the perineum, palms, and crown. Then slowly raise the arms, palms facing each other, to chest height, keeping the elbows relaxed and sunk. Rotate the arms slowly until the palms are facing down. Be aware of the mideyebrow. Feel your breath, and lightly contract your eyes and the round muscles around the eyes. Connect the perineum bridge by slightly squeezing the sex organs and the anus; do this a few times.

2. Rest. Smile to soles of the feet. Feel the Chi bubbling in the ground, as if you were standing on a hot spring starting to bubble up.

3. Be aware of your Tan Tien and expand your mind down past the earth to connect with the galaxy below you. Multiply the energy and bring your mind back to the Tan Tien. Gradually feel the Earth Chi being absorbed through the whole body; absorb it into the bones and body as though it were a rising steam or mist. Feel the earth force move through the center of the bones and enter the bone marrow; it rises from the calves and thighs (femur bones) through the hip bones, spine, scapula, arms, neck, and skull. Finally, swirl the energy around your brain. Remember: Tan Tien and universe spiraling.

4. Raise the index finger on each hand slightly upward. Then stretch your

Buddha
Palm

99

thumbs out to the sides and down, so that they end up pointing down toward the earth. This hand movement activates Large Intestine 4 (Hegu). Large Intestine 4 is found in the webbing between the thumb and the index finger. It is called the "eye of the hand" or the "Tiger's Mouth."

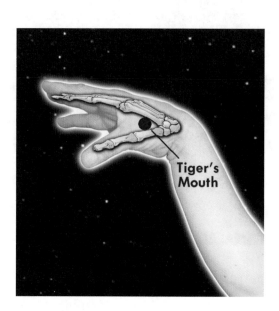

5. Slowly draw back the elbows and lower the hands until your palms are facing down beside the "eye of the hip" (the hip point or iliac crest), with the eye of the hand (Large Intestine 4) aligned next to it. Be aware of the Tan Tien (Yi), and expand your mind out into the universe. Remember: The hands act only as a guide to the flow of universal energy; if you focus on the fingers or the palms, you are starting to use your own energy. Use the intuition of your second brain (the gut) to be lightly aware of the area between the hips and Lower Intestine 4 on each hand. Feel your Tan Tien and the crown full with Chi. Focus on Tan Tien and the universe. This will activate the lungs and large intestine. Hold for thirty seconds. Gradually you will feel that the ascending colon and the sigmoid colon have been activated; you may feel some movement in this area.

6. Use your Yi to rotate your hands, moving the fingers from a palm-down, finger-forward position to a palm-up, finger-back position, and then finally rotate the fingers in to point the middle finger toward the eye of the hip. Keep most of your attention (95 percent) on Tan Tien and the universe spiraling, but remain just barely aware of the energy

flowing back and forth between the tips of the middle fingers, passing through the hip points. This will activate the pericardium.

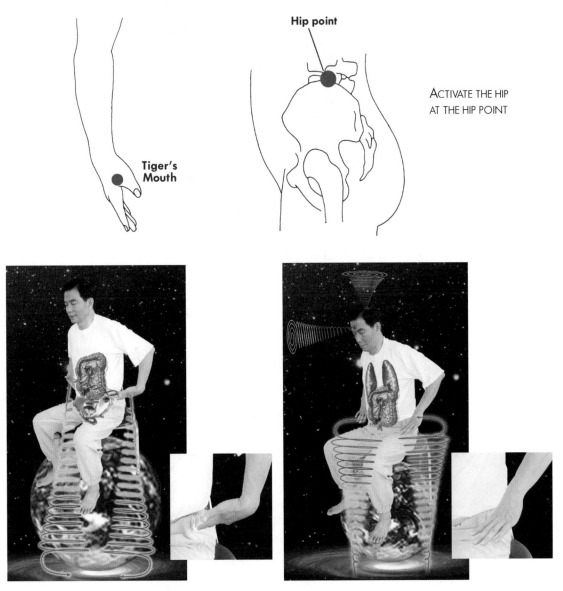

Hip point

Tiger's Mouth

ACTIVATE THE HIP
AT THE HIP POINT

ACTIVATE THE ORGAN ENERGY

7. Rotate the hands again until the fingers are pointing forward with the palms facing up. Align the knife edges of each hand (Small Intestine 3) with the eyes of the hips. Remember: Tan Tien and the universe spiraling. Be lightly aware of the energy passing back and forth between the two hands. This will activate the heart and small intestine.

Absorb the Heavenly Force: Marrow Washing from Crown to Soles

1. Extend your arms forward to chest height, with the palms facing up.

2. Bring your awareness to your Tan Tien, your crown, and your Personal Star above you. Expand your mind (Yi) out to the universe and connect to the galaxy. Be aware of the palms and the crown, which are connected to the galaxy. Slightly pull back (open) the index finger and slightly stretch the thumb forward and down to activate the Laogong point (Pericardium 8).

3. Feel the heavenly energy come directly to your palms, and be aware of the violet light of the North Star and the red light of the Big Dipper both shining radiantly.

4. Raise your hands above your head, as if you were holding a big soup ladle. Picture yourself holding the handle of the Big Dipper. Turn the "cup," pouring the light over your head. Draw this light in through the palms and the crown point, and feel it washing your bone marrow. Always stay aware of your Tan Tien. Direct the sensations down through the skull, cervical vertebrae, clavicle, scapulas, and sternum. Focus on your thymus gland to activate it, and continue drawing the healing heavenly light down through the rib cage, arms, spine, hips, femurs, calf bones, and feet and toe bones. Be aware of energy bubbling through the soles and up to the perineum and the crown.

5. Lightly rock yourself, as though you were riding a horse. This will help keep your spine open so that Chi can flow easily throughout the practice.

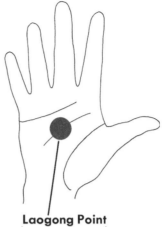

DRAW HEAVEN CHI
INTO THE PALMS

**Laogong Point
(Pericardium 8)**

HOLD THE BIG DIPPER

Absorb the Earth Force and the Other Side of the Galaxy

1. Bring the arms down to shoulder level. Rotate the arms until the palms face down.
2. Raise the index fingers slightly and extend the thumbs first toward each other and then toward the ground. Keep most (95 percent) of your attention on Tan Tien and the universe spiraling, remaining just slightly aware of the index fingers and the big toes. When you feel the Chi enter

*Buddha
Palm*

your fingers, fill the joints of the fingers and hands up to the wrists. Feel "tense but not tense" and let the Chi continue to fill the joints up to the elbows, up to the shoulders, and gradually up to the neck and the head. Allow Chi to flow from the toes up the legs to the hips and on into the spine and the rib cage, completing all the joints of the body.

3. Maintaining most of your awareness in Tan Tien and the universe spiraling, feel the palms (Laogong), the soles of the feet (Kidney 1), and the perineum bubbling. Activate these points, feel the earth energy, and continue smiling through the earth to connect with the galaxy and the universe. Draw in the combined light of these forces through the palms and soles and let it wash up through the center of your bones from the feet up. Let it steam and cleanse your marrow. Picture any impurities or illnesses dripping from your bones and draining down into the earth, where they will be recycled and purified.

OPEN THE INDEX
FINGERS

SECTION I CORE MOVEMENTS: CONNECTING TO HEAVEN AND EARTH

Grasping the Moon: Connecting the Heaven and Earth Forces (Right Side over Left Side)

1. **Open Position: Heaven Chi.** Holding the hands with the palms facing down, slightly raise the index fingers to open the palms. Bend the elbows and bring up the arms so that the right forearm is over the left forearm.

This practice uses the Empty Force; no physical contact is required, and the fingers must be tense without tensing. When you tense and raise the index finger, you will feel the Laogong point opening.

The left hand is under the right elbow, with the left index finger pointing up to Heart 3. The right index finger, held just above the Large Intestine 11 point on the left arm, points up toward heaven and connects to the galaxy.

The right index finger draws in the heavenly force like an antenna. The force flows up the bones of the right arm, across the shoulders to the left arm, and through the bones of the left arm to the tip of the left index finger. It then flows through the index finger of the left hand into the Heart 3 point of the right arm, completing the heavenly circuit. Continue cycling in this way. Hold the position and count to five.

COMPLETE THE HEAVENLY CIRCUIT (RIGHT SIDE OVER LEFT)

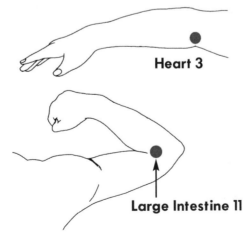

Heart 3

Large Intestine 11

2. **Close Position: Tan Tien, Earth Chi, and Universal Chi.** Keeping the arms in the same position, move both index fingers to point down. The right index finger now points toward the Large Intestine 11 point of the left arm, and the left index finger points down toward the earth and even further down to connect to the universe. Draw in the earth force through the left index finger, bringing it through the bones of the left arm, across the shoulders, through the right arm to the right index finger, and out into the Large Intestine 11 point of the left arm. Continue cycling in this way, completing the earth circuit.

3. Open and close three times altogether, ending in the open position. Hold each count for five seconds.

Grasping the Chi Ball: Tan Tien and the Original Force (Right Side over Left Side)

1. Turn the left palm so that it faces up, and lower your hand to the level of the Lower Tan Tien, with the pinkie pointing inward.

2. Lower the right palm to the navel, palm down, as though you were holding a small Chi ball between your hands.

3. Lower the thumb on your right hand to point toward the Laogong point on your left hand. This opens the eye of the right hand (Lower Intestine 4). Then point your right thumb toward the navel. Be aware of Tan Tien and universe spiraling.

Yin and Yang Palms

1. Separate your hands and extend them out in front of your body at navel level. The left palm is still pointing up and is drawing in the yang heavenly force through the Laogong point. The right palm is still facing

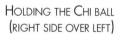

HOLDING THE CHI BALL
(RIGHT SIDE OVER LEFT)

Buddha
Palm

YIN AND YANG PALMS, WITH THE RIGHT HAND CONNECTING TO THE EARTH AND THE LEFT TO HEAVEN

down and is drawing in the yin earth and galactic force from below. Remember: Tan Tien and the universe spiraling.

2. Conclude by turning over the left palm so that it faces down. Draw in the earth force through both palms.

Left Side

Repeat "Grasping the Moon" (pages 104–106) and "Grasping the Chi Ball" (page 106) on the left side, with the left arm over the right. Hold each pose for a count of five seconds.

COMPLETE THE HEAVENLY CIRCUIT (LEFT SIDE OVER RIGHT)

HOLDING THE CHI BALL (LEFT SIDE OVER RIGHT)

Buddha
Palm

SECTION II CORE MOVEMENTS: OPENING THE BRIDGE AND REGULATOR CHANNELS

Activating the Throat Center (Right Side)

1. Keeping the elbows sunk, raise the left palm so that it is about one inch in front of the throat center (Conception Vessel 22), palm facing in. Then bring the right hand up so that it is about one inch behind the left hand, palm facing in. Align the Lung 10 point in the middle of the eminence of the left hand with the throat center. Feel the Chi go through the neck to the seventh cervical vertebra (C7). Continue smiling to the universe and connect to the universe behind your head. Hold for five to thirty seconds and feel the throat center activated.

CONNECT TO THE
THROAT CENTER

2. Slowly move both hands away from you, as if you were pulling silk. When the feeling of connection to Chi is diminished or the silk starts to break, stop. Be still and feel the beam connect the throat center to C7 and the universe.

FEEL THE
CONNECTION TO THE
UNIVERSE AT THE BACK

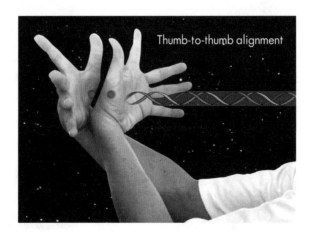

Buddha
Palm

108

3. Maintain the energy beam as you bring your hands in and out three times altogether, ending with the hands brought in.

Mideyebrow to Jade Pillow

Pull and feel the connections of the silken string of Chi flow

Activating the Mideyebrow Point (Right Side)

1. Be aware of the Tan Tien and the universe spiraling. Keeping the Lung 10 points of your hands aligned, raise your hands up to the level of the mideyebrow point, about one inch in front of the face. Beam the energy passing through both hands into the mideyebrow point and through to the Jade Pillow, a point at the base of the skull about one inch above the posterior hairline. Continue smiling and extending to make a connection to the universe behind your head. Hold for five to thirty seconds.

2. Using just a small portion (5 percent) of your awareness, move both hands very slowly out, as if you were pulling silk, maintaining the energy beam as you move. When the feeling of connection is diminished or the silk breaks, stop. Be still and feel the connection to the mideyebrow, C7 points, and the universe.

3. Bring your hands in and out three times altogether, ending with the hands brought in.

Activating the Organs

1. Keeping the palms and thenars (Lung 10 points) aligned, move the hands back down to the position in front of the throat center. Keeping the forearms horizontal at shoulder height, separate the hands so that the Laogong point on each is aligned in front of Stomach 13 (ST13),

Buddha Palm

just below the clavicle on a vertical line above the nipple or mammillary line. The middle fingertips should almost touch. You will now follow a vertical line down the torso to the level of the navel, stopping to focus and beam energy into key points along the way. At each of point, focus your Yi on beaming energy into the organs inside each position.

2. Beam energy from the Laogong points into ST13 and through the back to connect with the universe on the other side. ST13 activates the heart and lungs. Feel the change in your breathing as you activate the lungs.

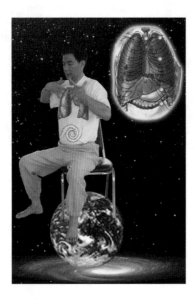

BEAM ENERGY INTO ST13

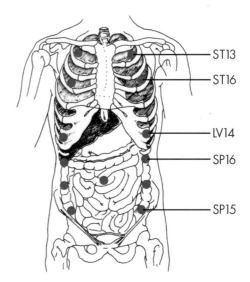

ST13
ST16
LV14
SP16
SP15

3. Move the hands down the mammillary line to Stomach 16 (ST16), about one inch above the nipple in the space between the third and fourth ribs. Beam energy into these points and through the back to connect with the universe on the other side, energizing and balancing the heart and the middle of the lungs.

4. Move the hands down to Liver 14 (LV14), two to three inches below the nipple in the space between the sixth and seventh ribs. Beam healing energy into the liver and gallbladder. Feel the Chi or the vibration of the palms activate the liver, and feel the energy moving inside there.

5. Move the hands down to Spleen 16 (SP16), just below the rib cage on the mammillary line. Beam healing energy into the stomach, pancreas, spleen, and liver. Picture the organs receiving Chi from the universe.

6. Move the hands down to Spleen 15 (SP15), on the mammillary line at the level of the navel. Beam healing energy from your palms into the small intestine and the Lower Tan Tien.

Buddha Palm

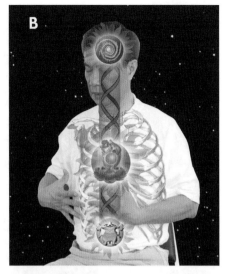

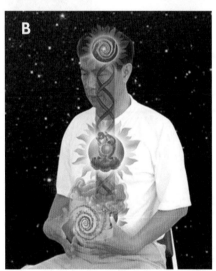

A. Energize and balance the lungs at ST16.

B. Energize and balance the liver and gallbladder at LV14.

A. Energize the stomach, pancreas, spleen, and liver at SP16.

B. Energize the lower Tan Tien and small intestine at SP15.

Grasping the Chi Ball (Right Side over Left Side)

1. Turn the left palm so that it faces up, and lower your hand to the level of the Lower Tan Tien, with the pinkie pointing inward.
2. Turn the right palm so that it faces down and align the eye of the right hand (Lower Intestine 4) with the navel.
3. Feel yourself holding a Chi ball between your hands and feel a Chi ball inside the Tan Tien as well. Feel the Chi balls connect to the Universal Chi outside. Feel the north (usually left) and south (usually right) poles in the hands. Feel the magnetic pull of the two opposite forces.
4. Lower the thumb on your right hand to point toward the Laogong point on your left hand. This opens the eye of the right hand.

HOLD THE CHI BALLS, ONE IN THE TAN TIEN AND THE OTHER IN THE HANDS

Yin and Yang Palms

1. Separate your hands and extend them out in front of your body at the level of the solar plexus. The left palm is still pointing up and is drawing in the yang heavenly force through the Laogong point. The right palm is still facing down and is drawing in the yin earth force from below. Remember: Tan Tien and the universe spiraling.

2. Conclude by turning over the left palm so that it faces down. Draw in the earth force through both palms.

YIN AND YANG PALMS, WITH THE RIGHT HAND CONNECTING TO THE EARTH AND THE LEFT TO HEAVEN

DRAW THE EARTH FORCE THROUGH THE PALMS

Buddha
Palm

Left Side

Repeat each of the Section II core movements, reversing the arrangement of the right and left hands.

ACTIVATING THE THROAT CENTER (LEFT HAND OVER RIGHT), PUSHING AND PULLING THE SILK AT THE THROAT

ACTIVATING THE MIDEYEBROW POINT
(LEFT HAND OVER RIGHT)

ST13
ST16
LV14
SP16
SP13
SP15

Buddha
Palm

SECTION III CORE MOVEMENTS:
OPENING THE FUNCTIONAL, GOVERNOR,
AND THRUSTING CHANNELS

Grasping the Chi Ball (Right Hand over Left)

1. Turn the left palm so that it faces up, and lower your hand to the level of the Lower Tan Tien, with the pinkie pointing inward.
2. Turn the right palm so that it faces down and align the eye of the right hand (Lower Intestine 4) with the navel.
3. Feel yourself holding a Chi ball between your hands.
4. Slowly rotate the hands so that your palms face each other in front of your navel.

HOLD THE
CHI BALL

5. Feel the invisible ball of energy between your hands. Allow the energy to push your hands apart, keeping the feeling of connection between your palms. When the feeling of connection begins to diminish, stop. Hold this position and reestablish the feeling of the Chi ball.
6. Let the energy, like a magnet, draw your hands back toward each other, until you feel as though you are squeezing and compressing the ball.
7. Stretch and squeeze the Chi ball a total of three times by opening and closing your palms in this way.

Activating the Outer and Inner Arm Gates

Buddha
Palm

1. Activate Wai Guan (Triple Warmer 5 or TW5) and Nei Guan (Pericardium 6 or PC6) by pressing two fingers against each point on both arms.

STRETCH AND
SQUEEZE THE
CHI BALL

2. With your right arm on top, slowly rotate the arms so that both palms face down. Cross the right wrist over the left wrist, with one inch of space between the hands. Align PC6 of the right wrist with TW5 of the left wrist. Feel the two gates activate each other like metal and magnet drawn to each other. Hold for five to thirty seconds.

3. Keeping the wrists crossed, slowly rotate the hands, turning the palms so that they face up. Now TW5 of the right wrist will be aligned with PC6 of the left wrist. Hold this position for five to thirty seconds, and feel the points activated. Remember: Tan Tien and universe spiraling.

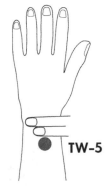
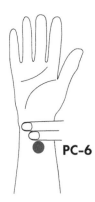

ALIGN AND ACTIVATE PC6 OF THE RIGHT WRIST WITH
TW5 OF THE LEFT WRIST

Opening the Functional Channel (Right Hand)

1. Bring the left hand down to the level of the Lower Tan Tien, with the palm facing up and the Chi Knife (index and middle fingers together)

ALIGN AND ACTIVATE
TW5 OF THE RIGHT
WRIST WITH PC6 OF THE
LEFT WRIST

facing in. Lower the right hand, with its palm facing down, and align the eye of the right hand (Lower Intestine 4 or LI4) with your navel.

2. Feel the Chi ball between your two hands, and at the same time beam energy from LI4 into the navel point.

FEEL THE CHI BALL AND
BEAM ENERGY FROM LI4
INTO THE NAVEL POINT

3. Raise the right hand up the Functional Channel, stopping and aligning LI4 with the solar plexus. Hold for five to thirty seconds and feel the points opening and starting to activate each other.

MAGNIFY THE POWER OF
THE BEAM TO THE
SOLAR PLEXUS

Buddha
Palm

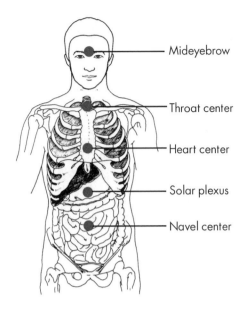

Mideyebrow

Throat center

Heart center

Solar plexus

Navel center

ACTIVATE ALL
THE POINTS

4. Continue to move up the Functional Channel to the heart, throat (Conception Vessel 22), and mideyebrow points. Beam energy from the eye of the hand into each of these points and, at the same time, continue to feel the Chi ball connection between the two hands.

5. Return down the Functional Channel in the same manner, starting from the mideyebrow and stopping to beam energy into each point: the throat center, the heart center, the solar plexus, and finally the navel.

6. Hold the Chi ball at the navel with the right hand over the left.

BEAM TO THE HEART CENTER

BEAM TO THE THROAT

Buddha
Palm

BEAM TO THE MIDEYEBROW

Yin and Yang Palms

1. Separate your hands and extend them out in front of your body at the level of the solar plexus. The left palm is still pointing up and is drawing in the yang heavenly force through the Laogong point. The right palm is still facing down and is drawing in the yin earth force from below.

YIN AND YANG PALMS, WITH THE RIGHT HAND CONNECTING TO THE EARTH AND THE LEFT TO HEAVEN

2. Conclude by turning over the left palm so that it faces down. Draw in the earth force through both palms.

Grasping the Chi Ball (Left Hand over Right)

Repeat "Grasping the Chi Ball" (page 106), this time with your left hand over your right. Lower the left thumb to point toward the right Laogong point.

DRAW THE EARTH
FORCE THROUGH
THE PALMS

ACTIVATE
THE CHI BALL
(LEFT HAND OVER
RIGHT), WITH
LARGE INTESTINE
4 POINTING AT
THE NAVEL

This opens the eye of the left hand (LI4), pointing it toward the navel.

Opening the Functional Channel (Left Hand)

Repeat "Opening the Functional Channel" (pages 115–118), this time using your left hand to beam energy through the points as you move up and then down the channel.

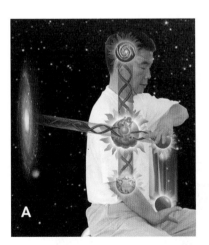
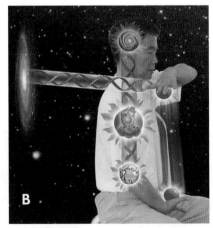

A. BEAM TO THE SOLAR PLEXUS AND HEART CENTER. B. BEAM TO THE THROAT CENTER. C. BEAM TO THE MIDEYEBROW, DESCENDING DOWN THE CHANNEL IN REVERSE, FINISHING AT THE NAVEL.

Grasping the Chi Ball (Palms Facing)

1. Open the hands with the palms facing each other at navel level. Feel yourself holding a Chi ball between them.

Buddha
Palm

119

2. Stretch and squeeze the Chi ball a few times in order to feel the Chi as a substance; open and then relax the palms as you squeeze.

HOLD AND SQUEEZE THE
CHI BALL

FEEL THE CHI BALL EXPANDING

Double Palm and Double Beam (Right Palm over Left)

1. Bring the left palm in to face the navel, about one inch away, aligning the Laogong point with the navel. Bring the right hand behind the left hand, aligning the Laogong of the right palm with the Laogong of the left hand and the navel. Both palms are now facing in.

BRING THE LEFT PALM TO THE
NAVEL

PLACE THE RIGHT PALM BEHIND IT

BEAM FROM THE NAVEL TO THE
DOOR OF LIFE

2. Beam energy through both Laogong points to the navel and through the body to the Door of Life, between the second and third lumbar vertebrae (L2 and L3). Hold for five to thirty seconds. Feel the vibration of the palms and the Chi beam penetrate through the navel and the Door of Life; feel them link together.

3. Raise the left palm to the solar plexus, aligning the Laogong point with the solar plexus. Follow with the right palm, aligning its Laogong with that of the left palm. Beam energy through both Laogong points into the solar plexus and through the body to the eleventh thoracic vertebra (T11).

4. Continue in the same way, with the left hand leading the right hand, to the heart point and the wing point (the point opposite the heart point),

RAISE THE LEFT PALM TO THE
SOLAR PLEXUS

FOLLOW WITH THE RIGHT HAND
TO FORM THE
DOUBLE BEAM

BEAM INTO THE HEART CENTER
AND THROUGH THE WING POINT

BEAM INTO
THE THROAT CENTER AND
THROUGH C7

BEAM INTO THE MIDEYEBROW
AND THROUGH THE BASE OF THE
SKULL

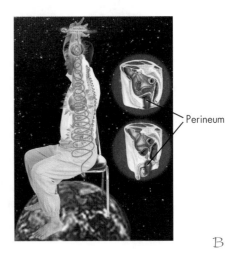

Perineum

BEAM INTO THE CROWN AND
THROUGH THE PERINEUM

the throat point and the seventh cervical vertebra (C7), and the mideye-brow point and Jade Pillow (at the base of the skull about one inch above the posterior hairline). Always remember: Tan Tien and the universe spiraling.

5. The final point for the double Chi beam is the crown point. When you reach the crown, lightly spiral the palms and feel the Chi slowly penetrate deep into the body, reaching the perineum. This will also open the Thrusting Channel. This might take a longer time; try a thirty- to sixty-second count.

6. Return down the front, point by point in the same way, leading with the left hand.

7. Go up and down this way three times. The double palm and beam activate both the Functional and Governor Channels. The energy beam passes all the way through the body at each point.

Grasping the Chi Ball (Palms Facing)

1. Separate the hands and slowly extend the arms in front of you at navel level, palms facing each other. Feel yourself holding a Chi ball.

2. Stretch and squeeze the Chi ball three times, as before. Remember: Tan Tien and universe spiraling.

SQUEEZE THE CHI BALL

MAGNIFY ITS ENERGY

Double Palm and Double Beam (Left Palm over Right)

1. Repeat "Double Palm and Double Beam" (pages 120–122), this time with the left hand on the outside and the right hand leading.

 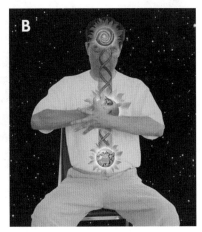 

A. Left palm over right, beaming from the navel to the Door of Life.
B. Left palm over right, beaming from the solar plexus to T11,
followed by heart center to wing point.
C. Left palm over right, beaming from the throat center to C7.

Activating the Earth Force

Rotate the hands so that the palms face down. Smile, and draw in the earth force through the palms, soles, and perineum.

Left palm over right, beaming from the mideyebrow to the base of the skull

Left palm over right, beaming from the crown to the perineum

CHANNEL THE
EARTH FORCE

SECTION IV CORE MOVEMENTS: ACTIVATING THE YIN AND YANG CHANNELS OF THE ARMS AND THE CHI BELT

Activating the Yin Channels (Left Side)

1. Turn the palms so they face down, and slightly open the index fingers. Smile to your palms and soles and channel the earth force.

2. Turn up your right palm and pass it just one inch below the yin channels on the inside of the left arm, from the palm to the armpit, without physically touching the arm. Feel the Chi moving.

3. Turn your right palm to face your left rib cage. Pass your right hand down the left side of your abdomen along the descending colon and then across the pelvis to the right side. This activates yin energy.

4. Pass your right hand up the right side of the abdomen to the level of your forehead. Turn the palm to face diagonally toward the left palm, and simultaneously rotate the left hand so that its palm faces up at the level of the navel. Project the Chi from the right palm to the left for thirty to sixty seconds, vibrating the right palm and feeling the left palm picking up the Chi. Keep the palms open and relaxed.

5. Point the ring finger on the right hand toward the left palm. Making very small circles with the right ring finger (Triple Warmer Channel), project Chi to the left palm for thirty to sixty seconds. Then return the right index finger to neutral position.

Buddha
Palm

124

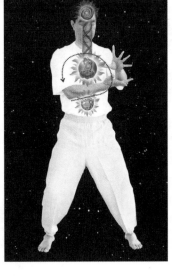

CHANNEL THE
EARTH FORCE

ACTIVATE THE YIN ENERGY FROM THE
PALM TO THE PELVIS

6. Point the left ring finger up toward the right palm and use it to project Chi into the right palm for thirty to sixty seconds. Then return to neutral.

7. Point both ring fingers at the opposite palm. Project Chi from both fingers toward the opposite palm for thirty to sixty seconds. Notice that the energy may meet in the middle. Then return to neutral.

RAISE CHI IN THE
RIGHT PALM

PASS CHI TO THE LEFT PALM

PROJECT ENERGY AND
BALANCE THE LEFT
AND THE RIGHT

A. FACE THE LEFT PALM DOWN, THEN LOWER THE RIGHT PALM TO COVER THE BACK OF THE LEFT HAND. B. PASS THE RIGHT PALM OVER THE LEFT ARM'S YANG CHANNELS. C. PASS THE RIGHT PALM ACROSS THE CHEST AND SCOOP IT UNDER THE RIGHT ARMPIT, FINGERS FIRST. D. PRESS BOTH PALMS FORWARD, RELAX, AND CHANNEL THE EARTH FORCE. BALANCE YIN AND YANG ON THE LEFT SIDE AND CHANNEL EARTH ENERGY.

Activating the Yang Channels (Left Side)

1. Turn the left palm down, and lower the right palm to cover the back of the left hand, palm down. Pass the right palm over the left arm's yang channels, on the outside of the arm, from the back of the left hand to the left shoulder.

2. Pass the right palm across the upper chest and across the right breast. Scoop the right palm under the right armpit, fingers first. Then bring the right palm forward, palm down, and press forward with the left palm at the same time. Relax and channel the earth force.

Activating the Yin and Yang Channels (Right Side)

Repeat "Activating the Yin Channels" (pages 124–125) and "Activating the Yang Channels" (above), this time on the right side of the body.

Activating the Yin and Yang Channels (Other Fingers)

Repeat "Activating the Yin Channels" (pages 124–125) and "Activating the Yang Channels" (above) with the other fingers and channels in the following order:

Buddha
Palm

BALANCE YIN AND YANG ON THE RIGHT SIDE AND CHANNEL EARTH ENERGY

Index finger (Large Intestine Channel)
Thumb (Lung Channel)
Pinkie finger (Heart Channel)
Middle finger (Pericardium Channel)

As you grow practiced with one-finger art, activate the Laogong point as you activate the yin and yang channels

Activating the Chi Belt (Right Foot Forward)

1. Step forward with the right foot. Cover the navel with your right palm and the Door of Life with your left palm. Feel the Chi beam penetrate from palm to palm.
2. Turn your hips to the right and shift your weight to your right leg. At the same time, move your right palm to the Door of Life and your left

palm to your right hip in a sweeping manner. Note that the palms face the Chi belt.

3. Repeat steps 1 and 2 three times altogether.

Activating the Chi Belt (Left Foot Forward)

Repeat the exercise as described for the right foot, but now with the left foot forward and reversing the right and left hands.

Channel the Earth Force

Rotate the hands so that the palms face down. Smile, and draw in the earth force through the palms, soles, and perineum.

BUDDHA PALM CLOSING MOVEMENTS

The closing movements balance organ energy while activating the Chi channels. Hold the arms extended forward, with the palms facing down, at solar plexus level. Hold each stage for a count of five seconds.

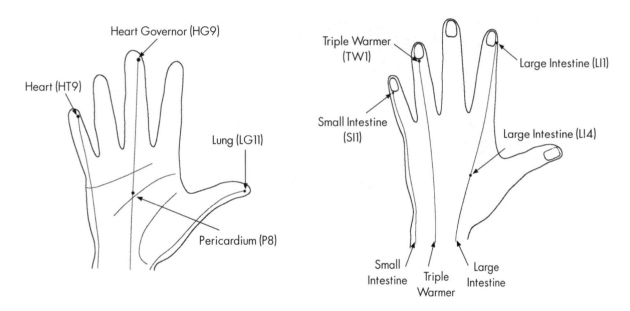

THE POINTS OF THE HAND

Index Fingers

1. Tense all the fingers and feel the Chi filling all the joints.
2. Open the index fingers by raising them up, while keeping the rest of the fingers level. The tension should be like that of the strings of a well-tuned musical instrument. When the fingers are lightly tense, Heaven Chi will be drawn in through the index fingers.
3. Relax the hands and bring the index fingers back to the neutral position, level with the other fingers.
4. Stretch out and tense all the fingers again. Press the index fingers down so that they point toward the earth and down to the universe. Keep the

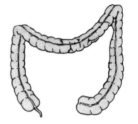

Large intestine

ACTIVATE THE INDEX FINGERS FOR HEAVEN CHI BY BRINGING THEM UP

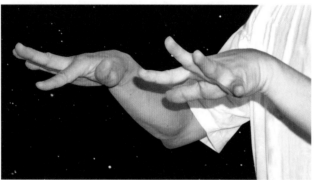

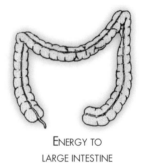

ENERGY TO
LARGE INTESTINE

ACTIVATE THE INDEX FINGERS FOR EARTH CHI BY POINTING THEM DOWN

other fingers level. Draw in Earth Chi through the index fingers and circulate it through the body.

5. Bring the index fingers back to neutral and relax your hands.

6. Once again open the index fingers by raising them, keeping the rest of the fingers level. Draw in Heaven Chi through the index fingers.

7. Bring the index fingers back to neutral and relax your hands.

Ring Fingers

1. Stretch the ring fingers down toward the earth, keeping the rest of the fingers level. Draw in Earth Chi through the ring fingers and circulate it through the body.

2. Bring the ring fingers back to neutral and relax your hands.

3. Once again open the index fingers by raising them, keeping the rest of the fingers level. Draw in Heaven Chi through the index fingers.

4. Bring the index fingers back to neutral and relax your hands.

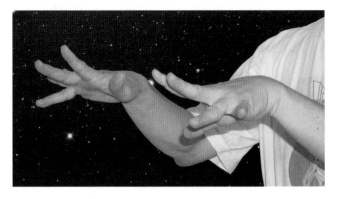
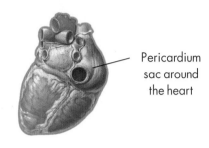

Pericardium sac around the heart

DRAW EARTH CHI THROUGH THE RING FINGERS

Thumbs

1. Stretch your thumbs out and down toward the earth, keeping the rest of the fingers level. Draw in Earth Chi through the thumbs and circulate it through the body.
2. Bring the thumbs back to neutral and relax your hands.

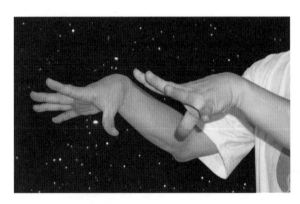
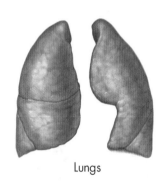

Lungs

DRAW EARTH CHI THROUGH THE THUMBS

3. Once again open the index fingers by raising them, keeping the rest of the fingers level. Draw in Heaven Chi through the index fingers.
4. Bring the index fingers back to neutral and relax your hands.

Pinkie Fingers

1. Stretch your pinkie fingers out and down toward the earth, keeping the rest of the fingers level. Draw in Earth Chi through the pinkie fingers and circulate it through the body.
2. Bring the pinkie fingers back to neutral and relax your hands.

Buddha
Palm

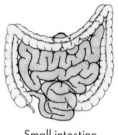
Small intestine

DRAW EARTH CHI THROUGH THE PINKIE FINGERS

3. Once again open the index fingers by raising them, keeping the rest of the fingers level. Draw in Heaven Chi through the index fingers.
4. Bring the index fingers back to neutral and relax your hands.

Middle Fingers

1. Stretch the middle fingers out and down toward the earth, keeping the rest of the fingers level. Draw in Earth Chi through the middle fingers and circulate it through the body.
2. Bring the middle fingers back to neutral and relax your hands.
3. Once again open the index fingers by raising them, keeping the rest of the fingers level. Draw in Heaven Chi through the index fingers.
4. Bring the index fingers back to neutral and relax your hands.

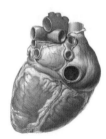
Heart

DRAW EARTH CHI THROUGH THE MIDDLE FINGERS

Crane's Beak and Swallow the Saliva

1. Form the "crane's beak" with each hand by bringing together all the fingertips, with the thumbs inside. Inhale and contract the sexual organs.
2. Move your tongue and suck the mouth to activate the saliva. Divide the

saliva into three parts. Tighten the neck and gulp down the first part to the center of the navel; force the second mouthful of nectar down to the left side of the navel and the third to the right side of the navel.

3. Raise the forearms to shoulder height, keeping your fingers pointing down. Slowly open the palms and begin to lower the arms to the sides, until the palms are facing each other before the starting position.

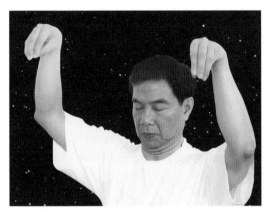

FORM THE CRANE'S BEAK

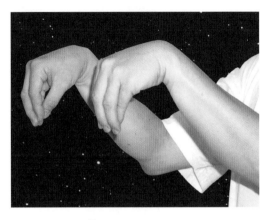

RAISE FOREARMS TO
SHOULDER HEIGHT

LOWER ARMS TO THE SIDES

AT THE FINISH, THE PALMS FACE EACH OTHER
TO COVER THE NAVEL

Buddha
Palm

133

Conclusion

1. Bring your awareness to the navel. Notice the quality and intensity of the energy generated and collect your energy at the navel.

   Men: Place your hands over the navel with the right hand on top.

   Women: Place your hands over the navel with the left hand on top.

2. Rest.

SIMPLE COMBINED PRACTICE

After learning the four sets of Cosmic Chi Kung, you may want to combine them all in a short and simple daily practice. This combined set, called Buddha Palm I, synthesizes the movements from the first three sets into one basic sequence. The movements are done on the right side only, so the entire set can be completed in ten to twenty minutes.

Combined Practice Opening Movements

Practice the opening movements of the Buddha Palm:

Combined Practice Core Movements

Practice a specific selection of core movements from the four sections:

Combined Practice Closing Movements

Practice the closing movements of the Buddha Palm:

General Healing Session
Cleansing and Strengthening the Body

As practitioners of Cosmic Healing Chi Kung, we ultimately cultivate knowledge and desire to share this knowledge with others. For this reason, this chapter assumes that you will be working on another person or a group of people. This form of Chi Kung is unique because it allows us to work on many people at the same time. You may use the techniques for yourself if you are not treating someone else.

The general healing session practices are to be done with every student regardless of his or her age or health condition. They will help cleanse and strengthen the cells of the body. If you have a hard time performing any of the steps in this chapter take some personal time and practice on your own.

CHI KUNG DIAGNOSIS: HAND SCANNING

Diagnosing the student's condition is an essential part of the general healing session. A simple and effective diagnostic tool of Chi healing is hand scanning. Hand scanning involves passing your palm over the body of the person you are working with, from one inch to one foot above the surface of the skin, and being aware of the energetic state of the various body areas. What you sense is the electromagnetic field, sometimes called the aura or energy body.

Hand scanning is an art, and it may take a while for you to feel confident using it. Practicing Cosmic Healing Chi Kung is one of the best ways to develop greater sensitivity in hand scanning.

General Variations in the Energy Field

The variations you may sense with scanning that have diagnostic significance are:

Temperature

Heat generally indicates excess, while cold indicates deficiency. However, some areas of the body are naturally warmer or colder than others.

Thickness

A feeling of thickness over an area would indicate excess, while thinness would indicate deficiency.

Wind

You may feel sensations of a wind or breeze leaving the body at various places. This wind may be hot, cold, or any temperature in between. It may indicate internal wind at a given location, or it may point to an area of the body that is leaking energy and needs to be patched or sealed. It may also be a positive sign that you are driving wind out of the body. In time, you will learn to discern variations of wind and their meanings.

Peaks and Valleys

Peaks in the energy field will feel like mountains or hills in the aural landscape. They may actually push your hand away. Valleys feel like depressions or energy vortexes drawing you in. They may also feel empty, like a hole or pit. Peaks indicate excess or stagnation, while valleys indicate deficiency.

Tingling

Passing your hand over an accumulation of sick Chi may cause your hand to tingle, feel prickly, throb, or even hurt. Such accumulations mark excesses of energy. Upon inquiry, the person you are working with may complain of pain in this area.

Scanning the Internal Organs

Each organ emits a different kind of force or aura through the skin. By passing a hand one or two inches above the skin, you can feel different sensations that reflect the condition or state of the internal organs. You need to develop the sensitivity to receive and identify the vibration or frequency of each organ. Practicing the Cosmic Healing Chi Kung meditations will help develop such sensitivity.

Liver and Gallbladder Scanning

Good Health: The energy of a healthy liver and gallbladder feels warm.

Negative Emotions: Feeling a charged energy come up to your hand is a sign of anger in the liver.

Overactivity: When you pass your hand over the liver and feel a rush of hot energy, this indicates that the liver is overheating because of toxins or emotional stress.

Underactivity: When you pass your hand over the liver and feel a dense and hot energy, the liver is weak, congested, and sick.

Lung Scanning

Good Health: Healthy lung energy feels cool and dry.

Negative Emotions: As you pass your hand over the lungs, make the lung sound (one of the Six Healing Sounds; see pages 17–18) and listen to the echo of the sound as it rebounds from the lungs. Sadness will feel like a deflating ball pressed between your hands.

Overactivity: Energy that feels dry and hot indicates an overworked organ.

Underactivity: Energy that feels damp and cool indicates underactivity or congestion in the lungs, which can lead to respiratory problems.

Heart Scanning

Good Health: Healthy heart energy feels warm and energetic.

Negative Emotions: Hot and charged energy indicates impatience, hastiness, and arrogance in the heart.

Overactivity: Hot, charged, and overly expansive energy indicates that the heart and blood may be overheating.

Underactivity: Energy that feels cool and less expansive indicates an underactive or congested heart.

Spleen Scanning

Good Health: Healthy spleen energy feels lukewarm.

Negative Emotions: Energy that feels damp and sinking indicates excessive worry.

Overactivity: The energy feels hot and damp when the spleen is overactive.

Underactivity: The energy feels cool and damp when the spleen is underactive.

Kidney Scanning

Good Health: Healthy kidney energy feels cold, but not too cold.

Negative Emotions: Energy that feels cold and chilly indicates fear.

Overactivity: When the kidneys are overworked or overstimulated by excessive exercise or improper diet and liquid intake, the energy can feel damp, sticky, and hot.

Underactivity: When toxins are blocking the organs, the energy can feel damp and cold.

THE GENERAL HEALING SESSION PRACTICES

The sequence of practices for the general healing session is listed below. It is followed by detailed explanations and instructions for the individual practices.

A. Three Minds into One Mind
B. Activate the Six Directions
C. Activate the Three Fires
D. World Link
E. Protective Circle and Chi Dome
F. Chi (Sacred) Water Practice
G. Empty and Fill
H. Clean with Green Light
I. Clean with Blue Light
J. Charge with Violet Light
K. Activate the Immune and Defense System

A. Three Minds into One Mind

As you've learned, spiraling the three minds into one mind activates Yi (mind-eye-heart power). With Yi power activated, you are ready to connect to the higher forces of Universal and Heaven Chi.

1. Place your palms together in salutation in front of your heart. Feel the Laogong points in your hands connect, creating an energy loop running from your heart through your arms and hands and back again.
2. Smile to the heart and feel it softening. Feel love, joy, compassion, and happiness. Smile down and empty the mind to the Lower Tan Tien. Fill the Tan Tien with Chi; spiral the Chi. When the abdomen is warm, it is full of Chi. The Chi can then charge up to the brain.

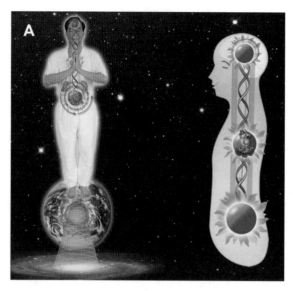

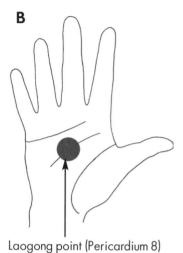

Laogong point (Pericardium 8)

A. EMPTY THE MIND DOWN TO THE LOWER ABDOMEN.
B. ACTIVATE THE HEART'S COMPASSION.

3. Lower the observation mind and the conscious mind of the heart to the Lower Tan Tien. Spiral the energy of the three minds into one mind at the Lower Tan Tien, building Yi.
4. Bring awareness to the mideyebrow.

B. Activate the Six Directions

Activating the six directions opens the body, mind, and soul to universal forces in all directions. You are now ready to draw in universal forces from all

THREE MINDS
INTO ONE

directions at the same time. This allows you to draw on the limitless universal forces, instead of your own limited energy, for healing.

1. Expand your awareness to connect to the universe and the Six Directions at the crown, mideyebrow, heart, and Tan Tien.

TRUST AND BELIEVE: TURN VISUALIZATION INTO ACTUALIZATION

C. Activate the Three Fires

The power of the Three Fires—Tan Tien Fire, Kidney Fire, and Heart Fire—will activate when connected with Universal Force. This allows you to feel the oneness and connection between you and all living things.

1. Smile down to the abdomen to create a burning stove near the lower lumbar and sacrum. Create a fireball behind the navel, just above the stove. This is the Tan Tien Fire.
2. Smile down to the kidneys, just above the sacrum and toward the back. Create a fireball there. This is the Kidney Fire.
3. Smile down to the heart. Keep the heart soft and fill it with joy, love, and happiness. Feel the Heart Fire activate.

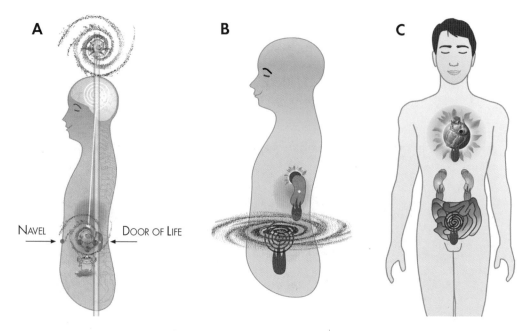

NAVEL   DOOR OF LIFE

A. ACTIVATE THE LOWER TAN TIEN FIRE.
B. ACTIVATE THE KIDNEY FIRE. C. ACTIVATE THE HEART FIRE.

4. Feel the three fires connect in a triangle. First the kidneys connect to the navel (Tan Tien). The heart connects to the kidneys. Finally, the Tan Tien connects up to the heart.

5. Fix the image of the North Star and the Big Dipper six to nine feet above your crown. See the cup of the Big Dipper filling with violet light, which gathers Chi from the North Star and the Universe.

6. Reach up with your left hand and grasp the handle of the Big Dipper. Pour the violet light down to your Personal Star (located four to six inches above your head), in order to predigest the energy of the violet light. Then let the violet light flow down to your crown and into the Upper Tan Tien. From there, the light flows down to your heart center and into the Middle Tan Tien or to the back of the head, down to the seventh cervical vertebra (C7) and the second thoracic vertebra (T2), and into the palms.

7. Breathe in slowly so you can process the awareness of the Lower Tan Tien. Feel a suctioning force and warmth (Chi). Continue to breathe in and be aware of the suction of the crown, the North Star, and the Big Dipper above you.

USING THE PERSONAL STAR TO CONNECT TO THE GALAXY, THE NORTH STAR, AND THE BIG DIPPER

D. World Link

World Link is the practice of linking Personal Stars, energy bodies, and the universe. It is a way for intelligent life force to return to its source, connecting both inward and upward. If you are working with a group, the energy bodies of all those involved become linked, forming one large energy body. Each meditator becomes an individual unit in an integrated communication link between the earth and the universe.

1. Be aware of your Personal Stars above and below you. Connect Heaven to Earth using the Central Channel.
2. Use Yi power to connect to your Personal Star above.
3. If you are not working alone, connect your Personal Stars and energy body to those of the people working with you. Think about the bright

light above the crowns of the other people. Start to spiral your energy to connect to each of them.

4. Instruct your student or students to create an energy or Chi body, which becomes the major connecting point. Use your awareness and ability to conduct Chi to counterclockwise spiral the collective Chi of the group to connect each person's star and create a group energy body.

5. The meditators become satellite links of a group energy body. Spiral and connect each person's star together and group the energy into one energy body. This energy body becomes an integrated communication center for each person in the group. We become the center of the universe by allowing ourselves to be the link between each other, the elements, and the universe.

E. Protective Circle and Chi Field

We create a Chi field to protect ourselves from disturbances and psychic attacks. Using Sacred Fire, we cast a circle around ourselves, creating an ener-

Soul, personal star, or higher self

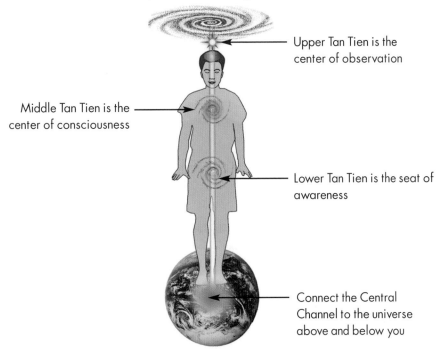

Upper Tan Tien is the
center of observation

Middle Tan Tien is the
center of consciousness

Lower Tan Tien is the seat of
awareness

Connect the Central
Channel to the universe
above and below you

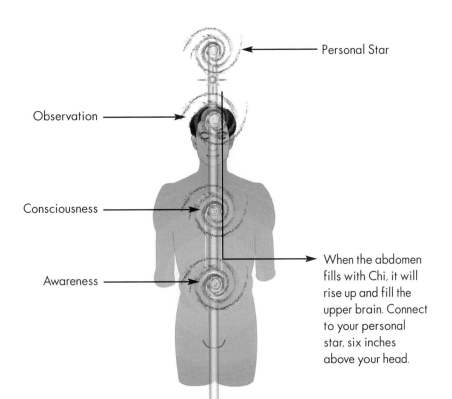

Personal Star

Observation

Consciousness

Awareness

When the abdomen
fills with Chi, it will
rise up and fill the
upper brain. Connect
to your personal
star, six inches
above your head.

General
Healing
Session

Universal Chi

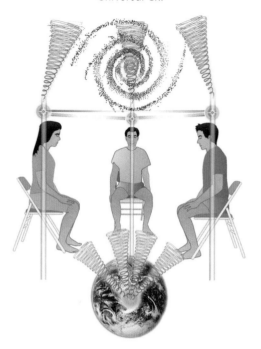

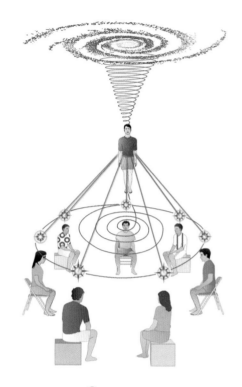

LINK WITH THE PERSONAL STARS OF EACH
MEMBER OF THE GROUP

CONNECT TO
A GROUP STAR

FORM A SATELLITE LINK
AND CREATE A GROUP
ENERGY BODY

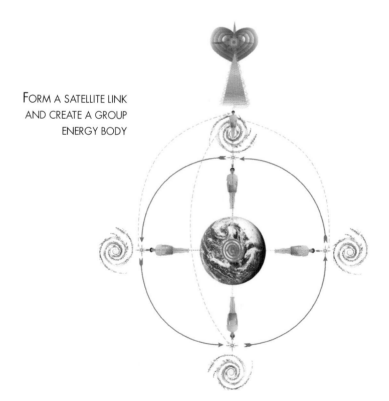

getic field of Chi. We create a dome of Chi above this circle, invoking the guardian animals—Blue Tortoise from the north, Red Pheasant from the south, Green Dragon from the east, White Tiger from the west, Yellow Phoenix from above, and Black Tortoise from below—to protect it. Finally, we activate the Eight Elemental Forces of nature and the universe: fire, water (ocean), thunder (lightning), lake (rain), earth, mountain, wind, and heaven. We gather these forces close to us and store them in the Chi Dome. In this way, we have available to us whatever power we need when we need it.

In Taoist practice, we create an external environment that parallels our internal environment. By connecting the Three Fires, we are able to have awareness of the Sacred Fire internally. Now I ask you to be aware that this fire also exists in the universe. With practice, you can learn to touch and use this paralleling Sacred Fire.

1. Be aware of yourself. Feel that your arm and fingers are big, long, and hollow. Reach to the universe, to the Sacred Fire. Let the Sacred Fire fill and pack your arm.
2. Use Yi power and the sword fingers (see the illustration below) to project this Sacred Fire outward from the fingertips and draw a circle of Sacred Fire on the ground around your house, your office building, and the room you are currently working in.

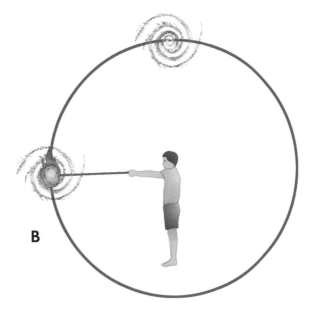

A. CONNECT TO THE SACRED FIRE OF THE UNIVERSE. B. USE SACRED FIRE TO DRAW A CIRCLE ON THE GROUND AROUND YOU.

3. Create a Chi Dome by visualizing a wall rising from the ring of Sacred Fire. The wall forms a perfect sphere above- and belowground, so that the aboveground section forms a dome. Set up the guardian animals, Blue Tortoise in the north, Red Pheasant in the south, Green Dragon in the east, White Tiger in the west, Yellow Phoenix above, and Black Tortoise below.

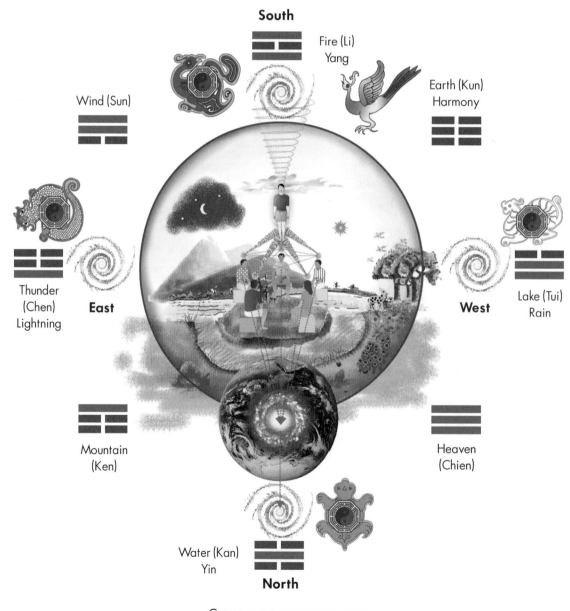

South

Fire (Li)
Yang

Wind (Sun)

Earth (Kun)
Harmony

Thunder
(Chen)
Lightning

East

West

Lake (Tui)
Rain

Mountain
(Ken)

Heaven
(Chien)

Water (Kan)
Yin

North

CREATE AND SURROUND YOURSELF
WITH A CHI DOME AND THE GUARDIAN ANIMALS

4. Call forth all Eight Elemental Forces: wind, mountain, fire, and thunder on the east, and earth, lake, water, and heaven on the west.

F. Chi (Sacred) Water Practice

We invoke the power of the Chi Water practice to cleanse and heal the body's sick, toxic, or negative energy. Cosmic Healing works on a cellular level. It is

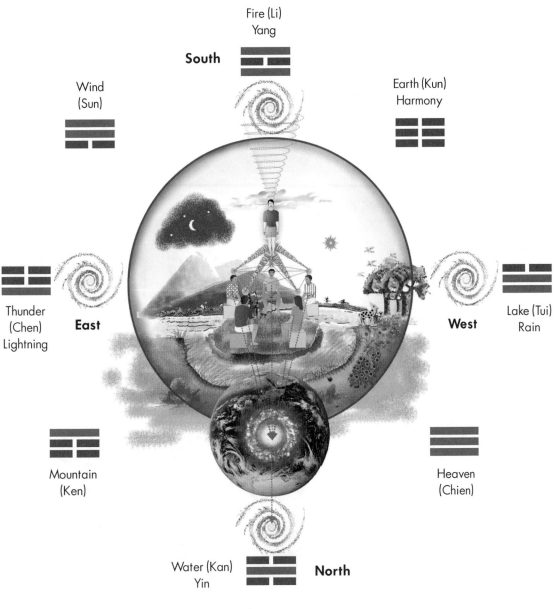

ACTIVATE THE
EIGHT ELEMENTAL FORCES

the water's "job" to carry the message of the practice to all the cells, where it will remain.

Theory

The following discussion of water and psychic projections contains extracts from the book *The Message from Water* by Masaru Emoto. The book advises us that water is "telling us to take a closer look at ourselves." Water is a mirror reflecting our minds.

Studies have shown that our psychic projections can access water at a cellular level, reprogramming its cells with the essence of our projection. For example, when we project Chi and love into water and then freeze it, it turns into a "normal" or well-structured crystal. When we project negative energy into water, it turns into an "abnormal" or poorly structured crystal.

When we project into water a nice, loving instruction or thought, like "Let's do it," the water picks up this vibration and restructures itself. If we project into water negativity, like the command "Do it!," the water acknowledges this accordingly. When we look into a pond, we see our image. When we drink a glass of negative-image water, its destructive energy enters our system and attempts to multiply.

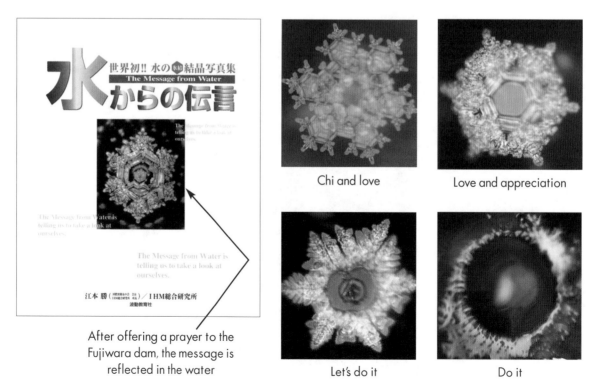

After offering a prayer to the Fujiwara dam, the message is reflected in the water

Chi and love

Love and appreciation

Let's do it

Do it

WATER CRYSTALS REFLECT THE PSYCHIC PROJECTIONS THEY RECEIVE

Research has demonstrated that if polluted water is filtered using every process available, it will still maintain its "polluted" vibration and unstable structure. In other words, it will maintain memory in the same way a computer does.

As we can see from these pictures, there is an enormous difference between natural spring water and regular city water.

Seventy percent of the human body is water. We must take in water on a regular basis to replace that which it loses to the outside environment. If the water we drink contains pollutants and antioxidants, it will eventually poison us. Likewise, if the water we drink contains negative psychic patterns, it will damage us. It is now quite clear that if we program water so that it becomes sacred, or filled with positive psychic patterns, it will have the power to reprogram the water within our bodies, to cause it to carry the same pure structure. In this way, we are able to remove oxidants, pollutants, and sickness from our bodies.

As the earlier photos showed, we can use intent to program a certain vibration in water. We can also use music for this purpose. Classical music

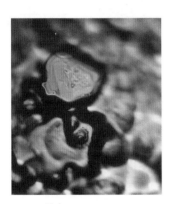
Tokyo tap water

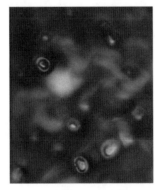
London tap water

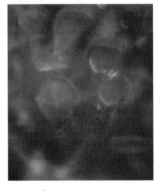
Paris tap water

Underground water from Northern Island, New Zealand

Springwater from Buenos Aires, Argentina

Springwater from Saijo, Hiroshima Prefecture

"You make me sick" or
"I will kill you"

"You fool!"

Heavy metal music

Thank you

Celtic folk song

Healing music

creates a vibration that synchronizes with our own health, whereas heavy metal music has a tendency to "shatter" cell structure.

The projection of our emotions toward other people has a similar effect on water. If we think negatively of someone, we produce a bad vibration. If we project kind, loving thoughts, the water structure becomes like a beautiful crystal. For example, if we love Mother Teresa and send this energy into water, a wonderful crystalline structure will be created.

Our mental attitude will be transmitted into the cells of the water contained within our own body. We must consciously practice inner work until having a positive attitude becomes reflexive. Sick water can be transformed into healthy water. Healthy water can be transformed into sick water. The key

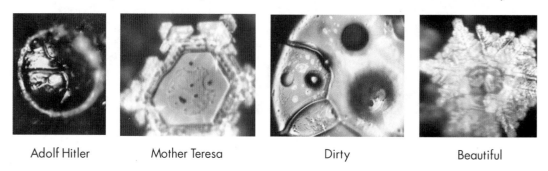

Adolf Hitler

Mother Teresa

Dirty

Beautiful

SICK OR SAINTLY?

Abnormal   **Normal**

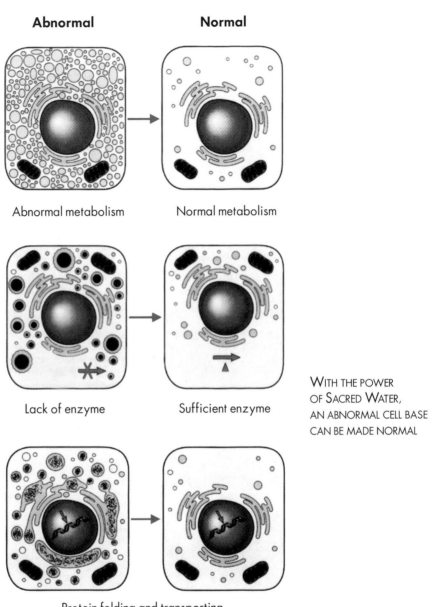

Abnormal metabolism   Normal metabolism

Lack of enzyme   Sufficient enzyme

WITH THE POWER
OF SACRED WATER,
AN ABNORMAL CELL BASE
CAN BE MADE NORMAL

Protein folding and transporting

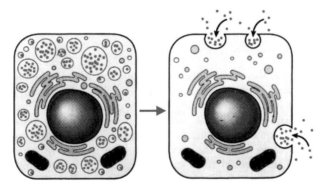

Ingestion of indigestible material

General
Healing
Session

153

is your intent and your ability to believe that healing comes from the nature of your vibration. Always be open to receive.

Practice

Invoke the power of the Sacred Water practice to cleanse and heal the body's sick, toxic, or negative energy. If you are working with a group of people, direct your energy through the energy body overhead and into each person's star as you guide them through the procedure.

1. **Prepare the hands and arms to receive Universal Chi.** Fold the ring and middle finger of the left hand into the center of the palm. Set a glass that is one-fourth full of water on the folded-down fingers, supporting it with your other fingers. Hold the glass in front of your body.

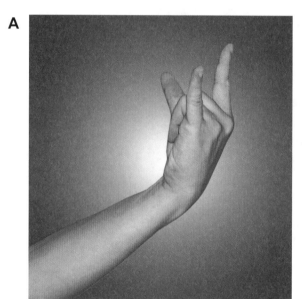 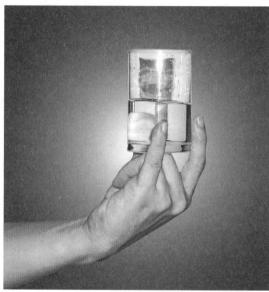

CHARGING THE WATER WITH YIN POWER.
A. FOLD DOWN THE RING AND MIDDLE FINGERS.
B. HOLD THE GLASS IN FRONT OF YOUR BODY.

2. **Prepare the sword hand to receive Universal Chi.** Form the right hand into a "sword" by folding the pinkie, ring finger, and thumb into the palm. Straighten and hold the index and middle fingers together and extend them upward.

3. **Fill your arm with the power of the heavenly pool.** Sense that your sword fingers and right arm are long and big as you raise them toward Heaven. Sense that the middle of the arm is hollow and the bottom is

FORM THE RIGHT HAND INTO A "SWORD"

TOUCH THE HEAVENLY POOL OF SACRED WATER ENERGY

sealed at the shoulder. Focus your mind's attention on merging with the primordial Chi of the universe, so that the energy of your thoughts will be multiplied.

As you make your request to the universe, asking perhaps to heal a specific ailment or just to energize the water you are making with healing properties, feel that you are touching a heavenly pool of Sacred Water energy. Feel that the pool is pouring down like a waterfall to fill your right arm. Compress as much Sacred Water energy into it as you can.

BLESSING SACRED WATER IN RUSSIA

OPENING THE THIRD EYE IN RUSSIA

4. Make a cross on the top of the cup. Place your sword fingers on the top of the cup. Ask for yin power: "Yin power and good fortune, come from the east. Yin has the power to dissolve all negative energy, all sickness and bad fortune." With your sword fingers, draw a cross on the top of the cup, saying, "By my request [repeat your request here]."

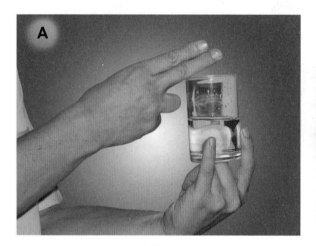 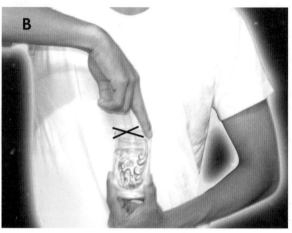

A. SET THE SWORD FINGERS ON THE TOP OF THE CUP AND CALL FOR YIN POWER.
B. DRAW A CROSS ON THE TOP OF THE CUP.

5. Charge the water to transform it into Sacred Water. Point the sword fingers into the glass of water. Smile and circle the sword fingers around the inner rim of the glass. Say, "Please carry out the order now." Repeat three times to charge the water with yin power. As you do this, project a good thought into the water.

CHARGING THE WATER WITH YIN POWER

6. Remove sickness from the cup and let it go to be transformed by the earth. Next say, "All sick cells, please listen: Clear, clean, and bright, this Sacred Water will take all the sickness away." Then use the thumb and index finger to pick up sick energy from the cup, without touching the water. Discard the sick energy down into the earth, where it will be transformed and recycled. Repeat three times. See the cells in the cup become clean, bright, and smiling.

PLUCKING SICKNESS FROM THE CUP

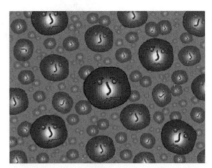
A

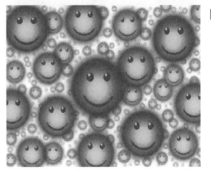
B

A. ASK FOR THE POWER TO SEE THE CELLS. IF THEY ARE TOXIC AND DARK, ASK FOR THEM TO BE CLEANED OUT. B. "CLEAR, CLEAN, AND BRIGHT"

RETURN SICK ENERGY TO THE EARTH

PROJECTING GOODNESS AND COMPASSION INTO THE CUP

7. **Fill the Sacred Water with compassion.** Hold the cup with both hands near your heart, and project goodness into the water, saying, "This Sacred Water will give me [or you] health, wealth, and longevity. Project love, joy, thankfulness, gratefulness, appreciation, and the energy of compassion into the cup.

8. **Drink the Sacred Water.** When imbibed, the Sacred Water will carry the message of healthy transformation to all the cells of the body. Use both hands to pass the Sacred Water to the student you are working with, or drink it yourself and/or in unison with your group. Feel the water go into all the cells of your body. Feel it removing the sick cells and purifying your body. You can also sprinkle the Sacred Water onto any area that requires healing.

DRINK THE SACRED WATER

G. Empty and Fill

The Empty and Fill technique empties the sick energy of the body into the earth and fills the body with healing earth energy.

1. Ask for permission to work on the student by communicating with his or her Personal Star.
2. Extend a "line" down from the universe. This line will act as a conduit for conducting energies. Extend the line from the universe into the energy body; from the energy body, a line extends into yourself and separate lines into the person you are working with. The line from the energy body sinks through the Tan Tien of each person and into the universe below. Through the lines, you connect your energy bodies in such a way that however you manipulate energy for yourself, the student feels the same effect.
3. Point your sword hand down at the ground. Visualize your hand and feet as being very big and very long, extending down to the ground.
4. Slowly inhale and bring up the earth energy. Bring the energy up to your feet through the Bubbling Spring points and into your bones. Let it enter all the bones, organs, and cells. Feel numbing, tingling electricity flowing in all your cells. Feel the earth energy blending with all the sick energy in your body.

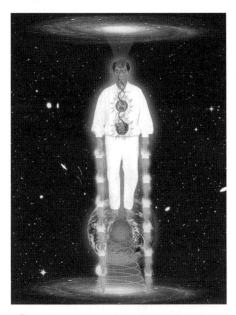

FEEL YOUR HANDS BECOME LONG AS THEY
EXTEND DOWN INTO THE EARTH

PROJECT YOUR LEGS AND THOSE OF THE PERSON
YOU'RE WORKING WITH DEEP INTO THE EARTH

BRING THE
UNIVERSAL CHI
DOWN AND LET IT
BLEND WITH THE
SICK AND NEGATIVE
ENERGY.
BRING IT DOWN
INTO THE EARTH
AND BURY IT THERE.

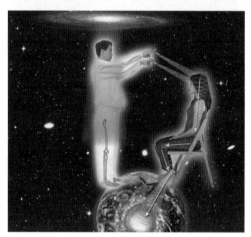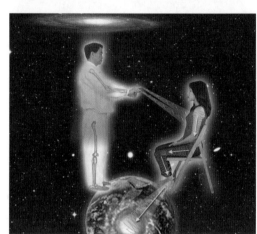

5. Turn up your palm up, then turn it back down and exhale, letting go of all the sick energy, the negative energy, the worries, and the burdens, releasing them down to the earth. Say to yourself or the group, "You must let go of all your sick energy. Let go of all your burdens. Let go of all your worries. Let them go down to the earth."

6. Repeat steps 3 and 4 at least three, six, or nine times. When people are very sick, you need to clean them thoroughly, performing this exercise more than nine times.

7. Bring the earth energy up into your bones once again. Inhale from the universe and into the earth. Let the Earth Chi enter your bones and pass from the bones all the way to your inner self. Feel the energy blend with the sick energy. Using Yi power, allow Universal Chi to enter through the crown and Earth Chi to flow in through the feet. Take a moment and allow this visualization to become actualization.

8. Exhale, letting go of all your sick energy and any negative emotions, burdens, worries, anxieties. Release them all the way down into the

earth. Dig a hole and bury them there; tell them, "Do not come back. You will be happy there."

9. Feel that the feet are long and extended into the earth. The hollow bones have been compacted with compressed Chi.

10. Once again guide the good Chi from earth up to fill your bones. See the cells as big as the stars and fill them with Chi to blend with the dirty and sick energy. Then empty them again down to the earth.

YOU CAN ALSO USE A TREE TO GUIDE THE CHI DOWN INTO THE EARTH

H. Clean with Green Light

The green Chi or light cleans the cells of the body. This is vitally important, because the cells must be clean in order for healing to take place. Green Chi "loosens" areas in the body; it is used to break down dirty or diseased energy, like a detergent is used for washing clothes or dishes. It is mild and safe.

When you carry out healing, try to "see" the cells enlarged and this green energy going in to blend with the dirty, black, or cloudy energy. See the negative energy emerge and let it go down to the earth.

Activate the Throat Center

1. Become aware of your liver and its green color. Smile to your liver to activate its energy. Become aware of the green forest in your Chi field and the green healing light that emanates from it and the universe. Become aware of the throat center and its connection to the green forest. Breathe the green light into your throat center and guide it down to the Lower Tan Tien.

2. Blend the green light from all sources in the Tan Tien, move it up to

BLEND GREEN CHI INTO THE THREE TAN TIENS; PROJECT THE ENERGY TO THE UNIVERSE, MULTIPLY, AND BRING THE ENERGY BACK DOWN TO THE STUDENT

DRAW DOWN THE GREEN LIGHT FROM THE UNIVERSE

the heart and the crown, and project it to the universe. Spiral the energy, letting it multiply.

3. Channel one direct line down to your crown, your palm, and any student you may be working with.

4. Be aware of the smiling liver, the gallbladder, the forest, and the throat breathing. Be aware of the green light in the universe. Let the light come in and blend in the Tan Tien. Bring the light up to the heart to blend with its compassion and then up to the crown.

5. Project the light to the universe. See it spiral and let it multiply.

6. Keep your Tan Tien Fire warm. Spiral in your Tan Tien and spiral the energy down to yourself or the student. Spiral at one thousand revolutions per minute, then ten thousand, thirty thousand, and sixty thousand revolutions per minute.

Cleanse and Remove Sickness

1. Raise your arms, with the palms facing the heavens. One hand remains still, holding the position and connecting to the universe. Move the other hand in a spiraling motion to spiral green light down from the universe. Spiral clockwise first. Multiply and then reverse direction, spiraling counterclockwise, bringing the Chi down to clean your community, your house, your work space, your body, the people in the room,

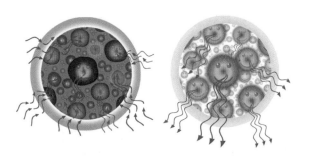

SPIRAL SICK ENERGY COUNTERCLOCKWISE DOWN TO THE EARTH. SMILE TO THE CELLS AND LET THE GREEN LIGHT CLEAN OUT THE SICKNESS, FLUSHING IT DOWN INTO THE EARTH BELOW.

and anyone you wish to send healing energy to. Fill yourselves with Chi. You will use this power to see the cells.

2. See the cells in your body enlarged. Let the green energy go in and blend into the cells, bonding with any sickness or toxins they may carry. See the green light carrying the dirty, black, or cloudy energy out of the cells. Let it flow down to the earth. Dig a hole and bury it there. Tell it, "Don't come back. You will be happy down there. You will be transformed into good Chi." Smile. Always smile.

3. Repeat steps 1 and 2 three, six, nine, thirty-six, or one hundred and eight times, depending on how much sick energy you are dealing with in your body. These numbers are a guide; they are not set in stone. If you or someone you're treating is very ill, keep going until you have facilitated positive change. You may need multiple sessions to accomplish your goal.

I. Clean with Blue Light

Blue Chi or light is like cold water. It has an inhibiting or cooling effect and the yin power to dissolve all kinds of negative energy and sickness.

Activate the Throat Center

1. Be aware of the blue kidney light. Smile to the kidneys and activate the blue light and water force within. Bring this blue light into the Chi Field and be aware of the water force within the field. Breathe the blue light into your throat center and guide it down to the Lower Tan Tien.

2. Slowly blend the blue light with the energy in the Tan Tien. Move it up

MULTIPLY THE UNIVERSAL
BLUE LIGHT; GUIDE
THE ENERGY FROM
THE THROAT, HEART,
AND CROWN INTO
THE UNIVERSE AND
BACK DOWN

and blend the blue light in the heart and in the crown. Project the blue light up to the universe, spiraling clockwise. Then feel the universe pouring the blue light back down, spiraling counterclockwise.

3. Channel a direct line down to your crown, to your palm, and to any students you may be working with.

4. Be aware of the kidneys, the bladder, the oceans, and the throat breathing. Be aware of the blue light in the universe. Let the light come in and blend in the Tan Tien. Bring the light up to the heart to blend with its compassion and then up to the crown.

5. Project the light to the universe. See it spiral and let it multiply.

6. Keep your Tan Tien Fire warm. Spiral in your Tan Tien and spiral the energy down to yourself or the student. Spiral at one thousand revolutions per minute, then ten thousand, thirty thousand, and sixty thousand revolutions per minute.

Rinse and Flush

1. Extend your arms into the air, with the palms facing heaven. Use one hand to spiral down the blue force. The other hand holds the position and connects to the universe. Let a big pool of blue light in the universe spiral down through your community, through your home, and then into your crown.

2. Let the blue light enter the cells of your body and flush out sickness and toxins, carrying them down toward the center of the earth. Dig a hole and bury the negative energy. Tell it, "Don't come back. You will be happy down there. You will be transformed into good Chi."

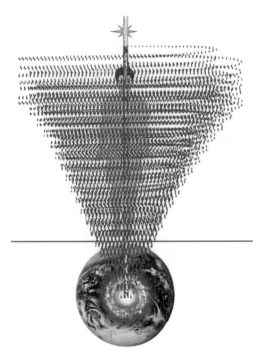

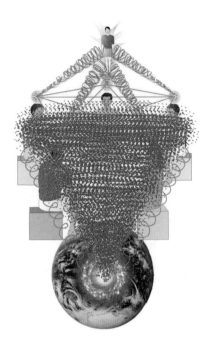

DRAW THE BLUE LIGHT FROM THE UNIVERSE; RINSE CLEAN AND REMOVE SICKNESS

BLUE LIGHT FLUSHES OUT SICKNESS AND TOXINS AND RETURNS THEM TO THE EARTH

3. Repeat steps 1 and 2 six, nine, or eighteen times. For people who are very sick, who have cancer, or who may be terminally ill, you can do this thirty-six, seventy-two, or one hundred and eight times.

J. Charge with Violet Light

1. Turning the three minds into one mind, go deep into the empty spaces of the cells and deep into the chromosomes, magnifying the space as you enter into the DNA. The empty space is the Wu Chi (the Place of Nothingness). When you enter this stage, you turn the subconsciousness into consciousness, and you can talk to your body and cells. You can change the programming of DNA and RNA.

2. Be aware of your crown, where Tan Tien Chi and negative Chi combine. See violet light. Extend a violet light up to the universe. See the North Star and the Big Dipper. Tell the student to hold an arm in the air, so that he or she can funnel the Chi into their Personal Star. Bring the North Star and the Big Dipper down; hold the handle of the Big Dipper and pour the violet light over the student's Personal Star.

CONNECT WITH THE NORTH STAR TO RECEIVE THE VIOLET LIGHT

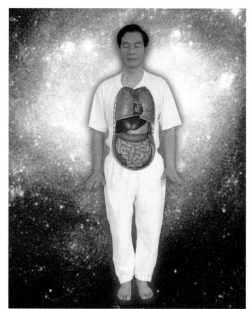

THE PRACTITIONER CONNECTS WITH
UNIVERSAL VIOLET LIGHT

3. Pause to let the higher cells of the brain reprogram the violet light to suit the specific needs of whoever is receiving this energy. Then spiral the violet light down through the cells of the brain and down through the cells of the whole body.

PAUSE TO REPROGRAM THE VIOLET LIGHT AT THE STUDENT'S
PERSONAL STAR

LEAD THE STUDENT AND GUIDE HIM OR HER. TELL HIM OR HER TO FOCUS ON THE
PART OF THE BODY THAT YOU ARE WORKING ON.

4. Ask for the power to see into the cells of the brain. Ask the student to move his or her hands to cover the brain. Say, "Brain cells, listen to this command: Sickness go away. Fill with violet light, clear, clean, and bright, and return to normal function."

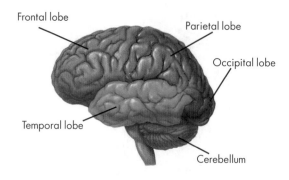

Frontal lobe
Parietal lobe
Occipital lobe
Temporal lobe
Cerebellum

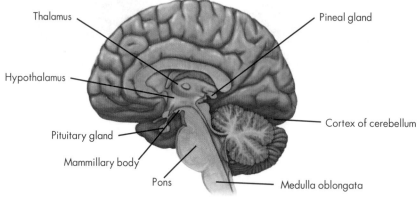

Thalamus
Pineal gland
Hypothalamus
Pituitary gland
Mammillary body
Pons
Cortex of cerebellum
Medulla oblongata

BRAIN: "FILL WITH VIOLET LIGHT, CLEAR, CLEAN, AND BRIGHT,
AND RETURN TO NORMAL FUNCTION."

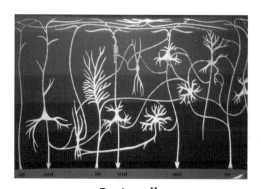

Brain cells

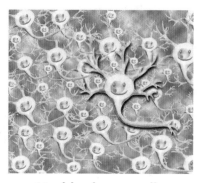

Healthy, happy cells

"INTENT" TO HEAL

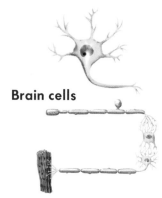

Brain cells

General
Healing
Session

5. Ask for the power to see the cells of the sense organs. Ask the student to move his or her hands to cover the sense organs. Say, "Eyes, ears, nose, tongue, and mouth cells, listen to this command: Sickness go away. Fill with violet light, clear, clean, and bright, and return to normal function."

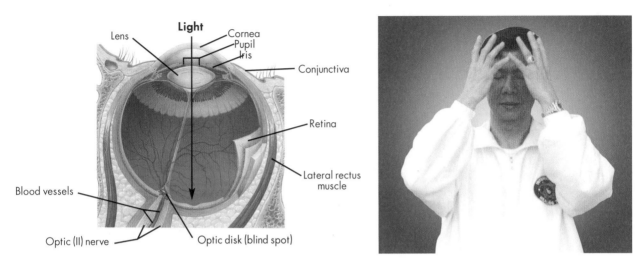

EYES: "FILL WITH VIOLET LIGHT, CLEAR, CLEAN, AND BRIGHT, AND RETURN TO NORMAL FUNCTION."

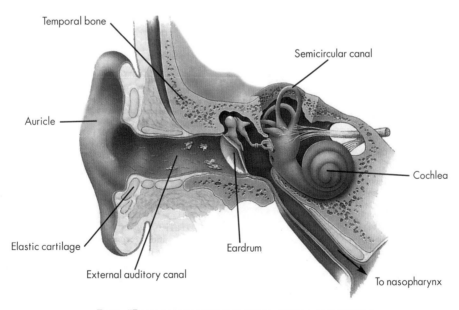

EARS: "FILL WITH VIOLET LIGHT, CLEAR, CLEAN, AND BRIGHT, AND RETURN TO NORMAL FUNCTION."

6. Move your hands down to your throat center and say, "Thyroid, parathyroid, and thymus glands, listen to this command: Fill with violet light, clear, clean, and bright, and return to normal function." Be sure to share this with the student.

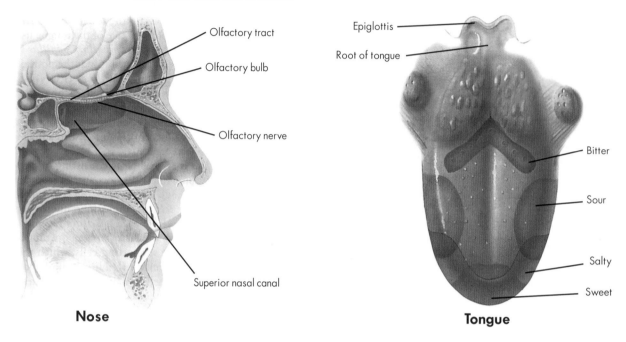

Nose

Olfactory tract
Olfactory bulb
Olfactory nerve
Superior nasal canal

Tongue

Epiglottis
Root of tongue
Bitter
Sour
Salty
Sweet

NOSE AND TONGUE: "FILL WITH VIOLET LIGHT, CLEAR, CLEAN, AND BRIGHT, AND RETURN TO NORMAL FUNCTION."

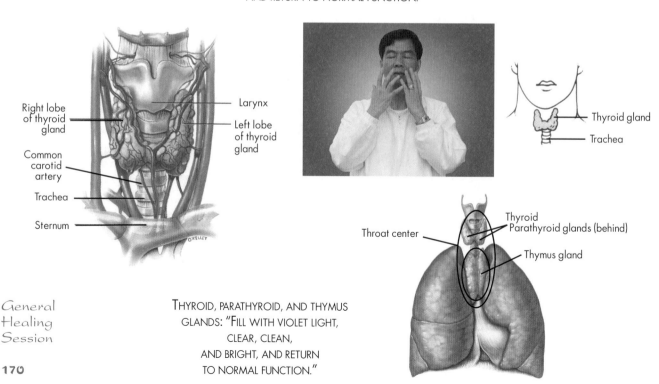

Right lobe of thyroid gland
Common carotid artery
Trachea
Sternum
Larynx
Left lobe of thyroid gland

Thyroid gland
Trachea

Throat center
Thyroid
Parathyroid glands (behind)
Thymus gland

THYROID, PARATHYROID, AND THYMUS GLANDS: "FILL WITH VIOLET LIGHT, CLEAR, CLEAN, AND BRIGHT, AND RETURN TO NORMAL FUNCTION."

7. Move your hands to the heart and the lungs of the student. Ask for the power to see the cells of the heart and lungs. Tell them, "Lungs and heart cells, listen to this command." If there is no sickness, cleanse them with violet light. If there is sickness, tell it, "Go away. Fill with violet light, clear, clean, and bright, and return to normal function." Make sure that you say this part aloud. Give the command in a very firm tone of voice.

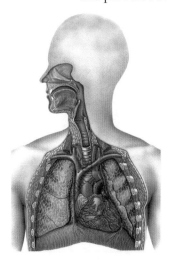
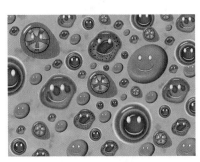

HEART AND LUNGS: "FILL WITH VIOLET LIGHT, CLEAR, CLEAN, AND BRIGHT, AND RETURN TO NORMAL FUNCTION."

8. Move your hands to cover the left and right sides of the ribcage of the student. Ask for the power to see the cells of the liver, gallbladder, spleen, pancreas, and stomach. Tell them, "Liver, gallbladder, spleen, pancreas, and stomach cells, listen to this command." If there is no sickness, cleanse them. If there is sickness, tell it, "Go away. Fill with violet light, clear, clean, and bright, and return to normal function." Make sure that you say this part aloud. Give the command in a very firm tone of voice.

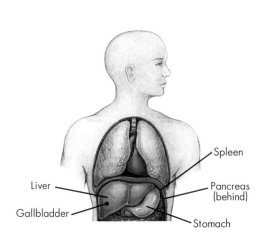

Spleen

Liver

Pancreas (behind)

Gallbladder

Stomach

LIVER, GALLBLADDER, PANCREAS, STOMACH, AND SPLEEN: "FILL WITH VIOLET LIGHT, CLEAN, CLEAR, AND BRIGHT, AND RETURN TO NORMAL FUNCTION."

9. Move your hands to the front of the abdomen of the student, covering the large and small intestines. Ask for the power to see the cells of the intestines. Tell them, "Large and small intestines, listen to this command." If there is no sickness, just clean them out. See the cells and clean them out with violet light. If there is sickness, tell the sickness to "go away—be clear, clean and bright; fill with violet light and return to normal function." Make sure that you say this part aloud. Give the command in a very firm tone of voice.

SMALL AND LARGE INTESTINES: "FILL WITH VIOLET LIGHT, CLEAR, CLEAN, AND BRIGHT AND RETURN TO NORMAL FUNCTION."

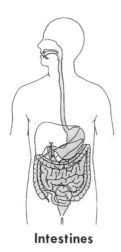

Intestines

Healthy cells

KIDNEYS AND SEXUAL ORGANS: "FILL WITH VIOLET LIGHT, CLEAR, CLEAN, AND BRIGHT, AND RETURN TO NORMAL FUNCTION."

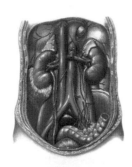

Kidney

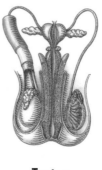

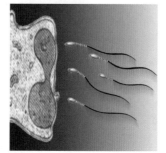

Testes

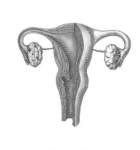

Ovaries

Egg

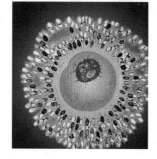

Sperm

Nucleus

10. Move your hands to the student's lower back, over the kidneys and sexual organs, and ask for the power to see their cells. Tell them, "Kidney and sexual organ cells, listen to this command: Fill with violet light, clear, clean, and bright, and return to normal function."

11. Gather the violet light and let it pour down and fill all the cells of the energy and physical bodies. See the violet light, and feel and see that all the cells are "clear, clean, and bright." Smile.

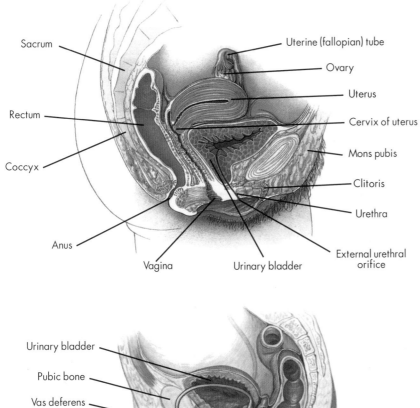

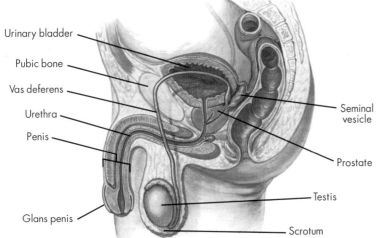

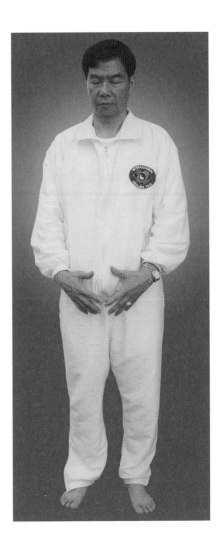

MALE AND FEMALE SEXUAL ORGANS: "FILL WITH VIOLET LIGHT, CLEAR, CLEAN, AND BRIGHT, AND RETURN TO NORMAL FUNCTION."

K. Activate the Defense and Immune Systems

The body has various mechanisms that combine to provide protection and defense against illness and disease. These mechanisms enable the body to produce various cells and other bodies that act against invading or unwanted substances. As soon as a foreign body is recognized, the immune system is triggered and acts to provide the most efficient means of eliminating the dan-

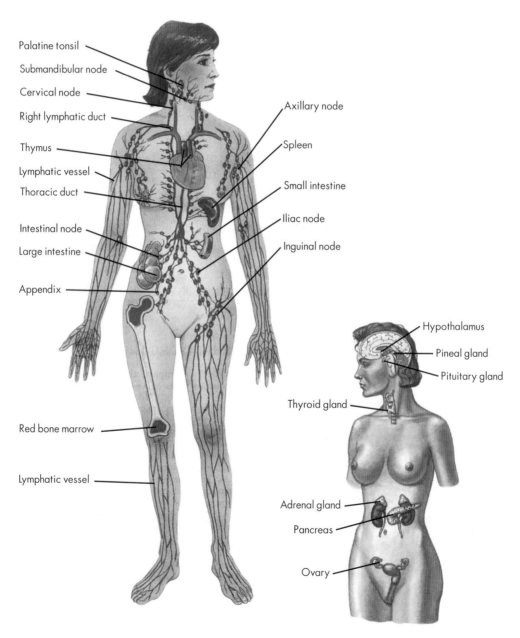

THE DEFENSE SYSTEM RELATES TO THE WHITE BLOOD CELLS, AND THE IMMUNE SYSTEM RELATES TO THE LYMPHATIC SYSTEM

ger and returning the body to a balanced state of health. A strong and healthy body will have good resources to protect itself from negative or sick energy. The aim of these practices is to help you realize the potential of true harmony within yourself. To activate the immune and defense system is to increase the production of red and white blood cells. To do this, we activate the bone marrow and the lymphatic system.

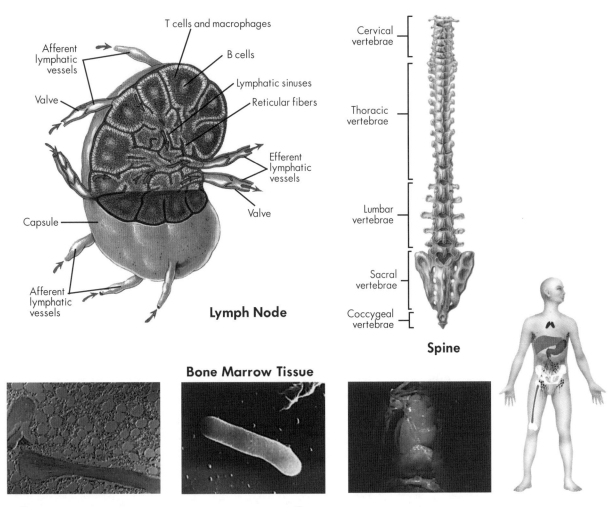

Lymph Node

Spine

Bone Marrow Tissue

BONE MARROW PRODUCES RED AND WHITE BLOOD CELLS. THE LYMPHATIC SYSTEM CLEANS TOXIC OR POLLUTED MATERIAL AND BACTERIA FROM THE CELLS.

A. Sacrum. The sacrum controls the bones and bone marrow and affects the production of red and white blood cells. Bone marrow produces the lymphatic cells (white blood cells). When the blood is full of Chi, it becomes lighter. Negative emotions make the blood thick and acidic. In a healthy body, blood cells can live up to ten times longer than they would in a weak or diseased body.

B. Bone marrow. Bone marrow is rich in fats and contains plenty of nourishment for the comprehensive production of the different blood cells: red cells for the transport of oxygen, blood platelets for clotting, and the various white cells for the immune system.

C. Bacteria. Bacteria are a common foreign invader, but they are only one of many invaders. Parasites, fungi, viruses, chemicals, mineral fragments, metal particles—these, and a great deal more, set the immune system to work.

D. Thymus gland. The thymus gland is perhaps the most important organ of the immune system. The vital training of the different T lymphocytes takes place inside the thymus gland. When precursor cells for lymphocytes pass through the thymus, they receive a program to convert them into T cells. When the T cells pass through the liver and large intestine, they become B cells and helper T cells.

The Defense System: Theory

We have obtained the illustration at the top of page 177 and the following text from the publication *The Body Victorious*, by Lennart Nilsson and Jan Lindberg. We hope that you find this short selection of material as informative as we did.

"The illustration below is a highly schematic and simplified picture of our immune system. *Top left*, the pale yellow 'house' symbolizes the bone marrow, where all blood cells are born. *Bottom right*, a solitary bacterium (yellow) represents the foreign invader that the immune system needs to combat. The light blue path represents the older defenses, with various feeding cells that tackle all foreign substances and also function as a kind of cleaning system. They deal with all the old, dead, and used-up material in the body. The newer special defense force, which develops later, follows the green path. Its cells are more specialized; they obtain their special training and reach maturity in organs such as the thymus gland and in the lymphoid tissue around the intestines and in the liver. In the lymphoid tissue, the yellow 'half-way house' (far right), the B lymphocytes are trained. These are the precursors of the large plasma cells—the pale green cells (far right) in the illustration, which produce the body's sniper ammunition, the antibodies (red and Y-shaped).

"The three paths from the thymus are intended to show that there are different types of T lymphocytes—among others, aggressive killer cells, helper cells and suppressive cells. All of them have specialized tasks to perform when the immune system launches a counterattack. The three blue paths of the

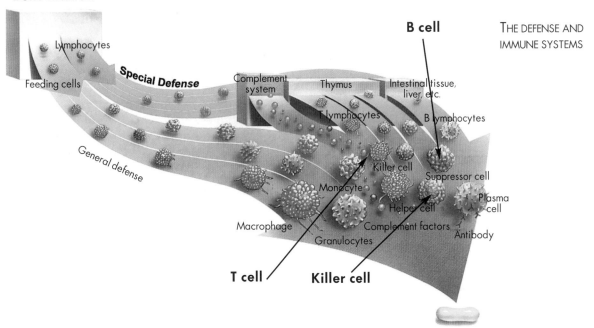

Bone marrow

Lymphocytes

Feeding cells

Special Defense

General defense

Complement system

Thymus

Intestinal tissue, liver, etc.

B cell

T lymphocytes

B lymphocytes

Killer cell

Monocyte

Suppressor cell

Macrophage

Helper cell

Plasma cell

Complement factors

Antibody

Granulocytes

T cell

Killer cell

Bacterium (foreign invader)

older defenses have three different kinds of feeding cells. First, the large and powerful macrophages (orange) advance on the enemy; then come the granulocytes (blue), smaller and faster moving, followed by the (pink) monocytes. The nuclei in the shimmering cell bodies are faintly discernable. In addition, there is an important complement system (middle), symbolized here by a multicolored range of small spheres flocking toward the foreign bacterium. These molecules play a large part in increasing the efficiency of both antibodies and feeding cells. In addition, they have the capacity to destroy bacteria by shooting holes in them. The complement factors are produced in many different cells in the body."

Chi Kung has a very strong effect against viruses. Altough medical science is struggling to discover a medicine that will kill them, Chi Kung practice is able to prevent them from occurring in the first place. Whether we are sick or healthy, we all need our defense system to be in good shape.

Defense System Practice

1. Work on yourself first to activate your sacrum. Touch the sacrum. Feel your fingers grow long and penetrate into the marrow. Feel that the sacrum is as big as the universe. See the eight holes in the bone, and visualize them breathing. Feel red and yellow light enter the sacrum.

General Healing Session

Guide it into the Lower Tan Tien. Blend the Chi in the Tan Tien. Move it up to the heart center and crown. Project the Chi to the universe; let it blend and multiply.

2. Open a direct channel down to the student and a separate channel to your palm. Project the student's feet down to the earth and connect to the earth's core.

3. Breathe and compress the Chi into the bones. Feel the Chi begin to rise up the spine and into your mideyebrow and temple bones. When you feel that there is enough Chi, project it out to the universe, multiply it, and spiral it back down. Project it toward the student and ask him or her to touch his or her own sacrum. Rub your hands together until they are warm and touch your sacrum again. Picture the sacrum getting bigger and bigger, breathing into the eight holes. Tell the student to smile at the sacrum. Picture the Chi from the universe coming down to your sacrum and that of the student and then charging up the spine to the rib cage, the temple bones, and the mideyebrow.

VISUALIZE AND FEEL THE BONE MARROW FILLING WITH CHI

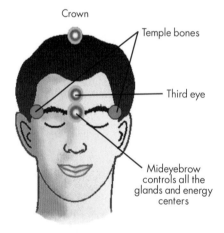

Crown

Temple bones

Third eye

Mideyebrow controls all the glands and energy centers

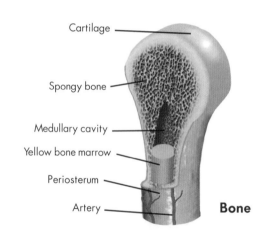

Cartilage

Spongy bone

Medullary cavity

Yellow bone marrow

Periosterum

Artery

Bone

TOUCH THE SACRUM, SEE THE EIGHT HOLES BREATHING, AND FILL THE SACRUM, MIDEYEBROW, AND CROWN WITH CHI. EMPTY TO THE UNIVERSE AND FILL AGAIN.

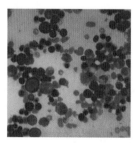

Bone marrow cells

General
Healing
Session

Third eye and temple bones are
aligned in a triangle

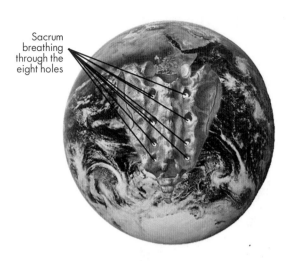

Sacrum
breathing
through the
eight holes

ACTIVATE THE
SACRUM; BE AWARE
OF
THE TEMPLES

Activate the sacrum until you feel the Chi rising up the spine
and feel it pulsing; be aware of the temple bones

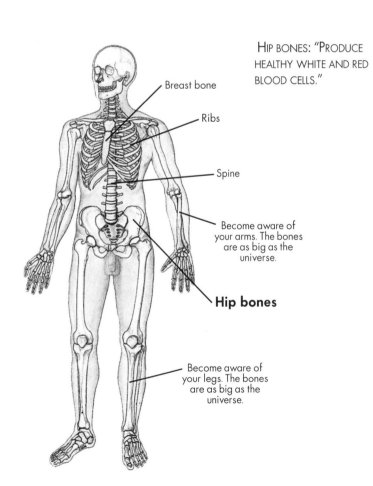

HIP BONES: "PRODUCE
HEALTHY WHITE AND RED
BLOOD CELLS."

Breast bone

Ribs

Spine

Become aware of
your arms. The bones
are as big as the
universe.

Hip bones

Become aware of
your legs. The bones
are as big as the
universe.

General
Healing
Session

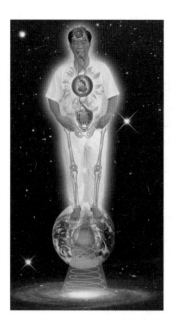

TOUCH AND FEEL THE BONES. LEAVING YOUR FINGERS THERE, LOWER YOUR MIND INTO THE TAN TIEN AND THE UNIVERSE.

4. Tell the student to move his or her hands to the hip bones. Tell the student to smile to these bones and feel them as funny, laughing, happy bones. Tell him or her to feel the electricity in the sacrum and bone marrow. Tell the student to pack and compress the Chi into the bones in order to revitalize and revive bone marrow. Give the command, "Produce healthy white and red blood cells." Ask the student to repeat the command.

5. Leave the fingers touching the hip bones and start to spiral in the Tan Tien until you feel the crown and the mideyebrow also spiral. Expand your awareness to the universe, and the universe will charge the hip bones. Share this with the student, either vocally or energetically.

6. Touch the middle part of the femur bone to help increase the production of healthy red blood cells. Feel the electricity running up the legs. Tell them, "Funny, laughing, happy bones, produce healthy white and red cells." Leaving your fingers there, bring your mind into the Tan Tien and universe so that the Chi can charge the bones. Feel electricity run throughout the whole skeleton.

7. Touch the humerus bones in your upper arms. Feel the electricity running up the arms. Give the same command: "Funny, laughing, happy bones, produce healthy white and red blood cells." Remember: Tan Tien and the universe spiraling. Leaving your fingers there, bring your mind into the Tan Tien and universe so that the Chi can charge the bones.

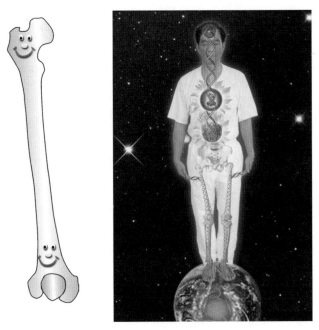

FEMURS: "FUNNY, LAUGHING, HAPPY BONES,
PRODUCE HEALTHY WHITE AND RED BLOOD CELLS."

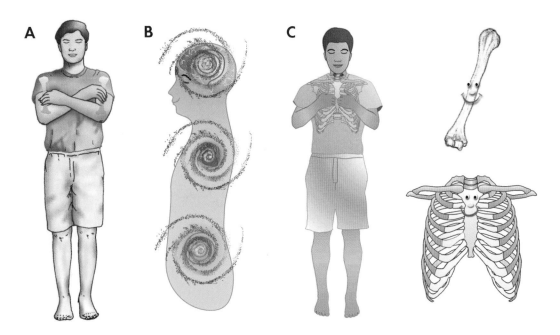

A **B** **C**

TOUCH THE HUMERUS BONES. A. HUMERUS BONES: "PRODUCE HEALTHY WHITE AND RED BLOOD
CELLS." B. TAN TIEN AND THE UNIVERSE SPIRALING. C. LOWER STERNUM: "PRODUCE HEALTHY
WHITE AND RED BLOOD CELLS."

8. Touch your lower sternum. Feel Chi penetrate the bone and spread out into the rib cage. Give the same command: "Funny, laughing, happy bones, produce healthy white and red blood cells." Then bring your mind into the Tan Tien and the universe so that the Chi can charge the bones.

You have finished activating the defense system.

Immune System Practice

1. The immune system starts with the upper sternum. Touch the upper sternum. Project your fingers deep into the bone and feel them penetrate right into the thymus. Activate the thymus gland. Gradually, feel the fingers rising up to the thyroid and parathyroid. Activate the thyroid and parathyroid and the throat center. Give the command, "Fill with violet light, clear, clean, and bright, and return to normal function."

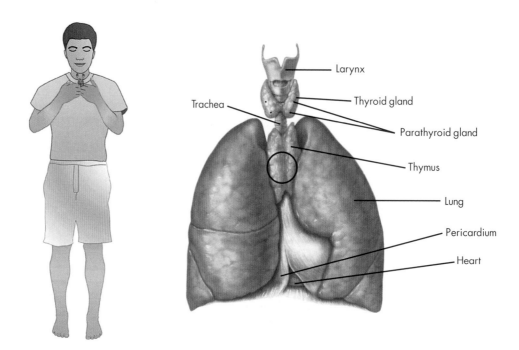

2. Move the fingers to touch both sides of the jaw bones to help activate the tonsils, the body's first line of defense. The jaw bone affects the lymph nodes beneath, which include the tonsils. Fill them with Chi. Give the command, "Fill with violet light, clear, clean, and bright, and return to normal function."

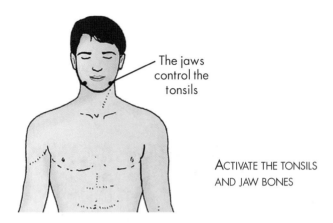

The jaws control the tonsils

ACTIVATE THE TONSILS
AND JAW BONES

3. Touch the mideyebrow and crown, which control the pituitary and pineal glands, respectively. Touch the third eye, feeling it open, and feel the light from heaven entering your brain and your body. Touch the crown. Feel your fingers reaching deep inside, and feel the Chi penetrating all the way down to your perineum. Give the command, "Fill with violet light, clear, clean, and bright, and return to normal function."

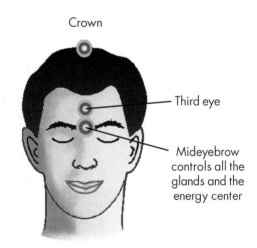

Crown

Third eye

Mideyebrow controls all the glands and the energy center

THE THIRD EYE, MIDEYEBROW, AND CROWN AFFECT
THE IMMUNE AND DEFENSE SYSTEMS

4. Rub your hands together until they are warm. Cross the hands on the neck and feel the lymphatic system has been activated. Cross your arms and hold your hands under your armpits. Picture the lymphatic system of the armpits as you activate the lymph nodes. Give the command, "Fill with violet light, clear, clean, and bright, and return to normal function." The lymphatic system of the upper body is clear, clean, and bright and the lymphatic fluid flows! Smile.

THE LYMPHATIC SYSTEM OF
THE NECK AND ARMPITS IS CLEAR, CLEAN, AND BRIGHT

ACTIVATE THE LYMPH
NODES IN THE GROIN

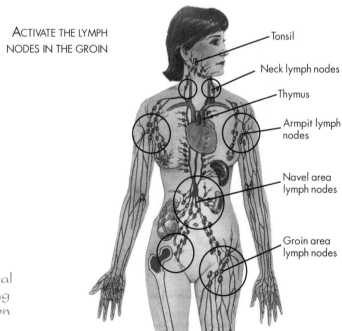

Tonsil

Neck lymph nodes

Thymus

Armpit lymph nodes

Navel area lymph nodes

Groin area lymph nodes

5. Move the hands to cover the groin area. To the lymph nodes there, say, "Fill with violet light, clear, clean, and bright, and return to normal function."

6. Bring your hands to the navel area and cover the lymph nodes there, saying, "Fill with violet light, clear, clean, and bright, and return to normal function." The groin and the navel area lymph nodes become clear, clean, and bright.

You have now activated the immune system.

Individual Healing Session
Treating Specific Health Conditions

Although each session is as individual as the person being treated, a few preparatory steps are necessary and will work regardless of the situation. We must acknowledge these steps so as to secure the safety of the people we treat and ourselves. In fact, we can treat the root of a person's ailment simply by doing these preparatory practices.

> Step 1: Create the Chi Field (using Sacred Fire) and call on the guardian animals (from the organs) and the Eight Elemental Forces.
>
> Step 2: Charge our hands and activate the Chi Knife. You will ultimately need to use your hands to break up and guide the stuck Chi, regardless of how it has manifested in the physical body.
>
> Step 3: Energize and activate the immune system. The person being treated must be able to produce the antibodies needed to fight the repercussions of toxic release.
>
> Step 4: Energize and cleanse the internal organs. They are the filters and processors of physical and energetic toxins.

Once these things are in place, the session will morph to the specific needs of the individual.

STEP 1: CREATE THE CHI FIELD

1. Gain experience by working with one person. Stand in front of him or her with your feet shoulder width apart. Hold your hands at your heart in salutation. Transmit your love and compassion and ask for the student's permission to help him or her heal.

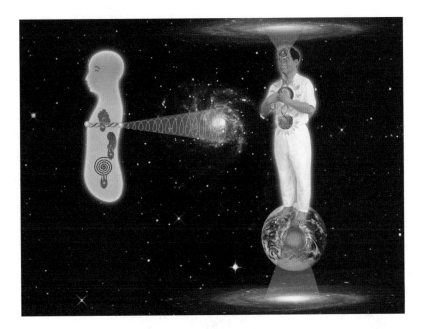

Use compassion, love, and kindness

2. Connect to the student's and your own Personal Star above your head and ask for universal permission to share energy with this person. Radiate your love.

3. Transfer three minds into one mind. Expand your awareness in the mideyebrow and the crown. Feel the Tan Tien, heart, mideyebrow, and crown spiraling. Expand to the universe.

4. Visualize the student's legs as being very long, extending down to the earth.

5. Activate the Sacred Fire and bring it down through your fingers. Use the Sacred Fire to draw a protective ring of fire. Clean out the room and make a big Chi field around you and the student.

6. Call the Eight Elemental Forces: water, fire, thunder, rain, lake, earth, mountain, wind, and Heavenly Chi. Call the guardian animals: Blue Tortoise from the north, Red Pheasant from the south, Green Dragon from the east, White Tiger from the west, Yellow Phoenix from above, and Black Tortoise from below. Feel that you are protected by the Chi; gather the power of all the mountains, rivers, streams, stones, and rocks

into the room. Activate them with lightning, thunder, and wind, filling the whole room with electrified Chi.

STEP 2: ACTIVATE THE CHI KNIFE

Since the dawn of ages and our descent into the material realm, we have constructed and used tools to facilitate the progress of events. We use tools to help nourish, protect, and amuse ourselves and to further our progress in attempting to understand the "how" and "why" of existential reality. They are an extension of ourselves that enable us to enhance, mold, and magnify our intrinsic nature as inquisitive playful beings.

CHI KNIFE

The Chi Knife is a simple yet powerful "friend" and derives as much power as we wish to lend it. The Knife itself is a vehicle with which the practitioner guides Chi to very small areas. We use either a physical instrument or our sword hand as the Knife. Its design may consist of any combination of the five elements (earth), which, when combined with universal (heaven) and cosmic (man) forces, provide a unit of energetic substance that receives and transmits magnification, purpose, and power in accordance with the human will that governs it. When we think, our brain issues waves of energy, and that energy, when focused, facilitates change. The Chi Knife, as a tool of that focus, reflects the precepts of a truly magical existence. When we learn to wield it, we come to understand that the simple things in life, like the knife, contain the same amount of power as state-of-the-art technology.

We can charge the Knife with yin or yang energy. We charge the Knife most often with yin. Yin is cold energy and is used for treating any type of inflammation, pain, or heat. It is used to break up illness. We charge the Knife with yang for strengthening, melting, or expelling. Use yang only in cases that do not present with pain.

Caution

When following these instructions for practice with the Chi knife, **use the sword hand** (shown on page 154) as your knife. Never use sharp objects near the eyes. The practitioners shown in the photographs are experienced masters holding ritual scalpel knives, which never actually touch the eye.

Practicing with the Chi Knife

Eye Problems

1. Hold the knife in your right hand (or the left, if you are left-handed). Hold the other hand near your body, with the thumb and index finger touching. Project the Chi Knife long and big, so that it is as big as the universe, reaching to Heaven. Feel that the bones in your arm are hollow, with their "bottom" sealed at the shoulder. Feel them fill and pack with the power coming from above.

2. Give the command: "Power comes from the east. This Chi Knife has the power to dissolve all the negative energy, sickness, and bad fortune. By my request, please carry out the order now." Wait until you feel that your arm and the knife are heavy and full of Chi.

3. Use the thumb and index finger of the hand not holding the knife to hold the eye wide open.

4. Hold the knife (or sword fingers) three to six centimeters away from the eye. Rest the little finger on the other hand for leverage and support.

HOLD THE KNIFE THREE TO SIX CENTIMETERS AWAY FROM THE EYE, RESTING YOUR LITTLE FINGER ON THE OTHER HAND FOR SUPPORT

5. Think or say out loud, "Chi Knife helps all eye problems." Cut up and down and sideways in the cross pattern "through" the eye.

6. Tell the student to move his or her eye to the left and then slowly to the right. As the student moves the eye toward the right, cut with the Chi Knife to the left. (Remember that the knife is used for *energetic* surgery and should never make contact with the eye itself.) "Slice" the eye toward the right side fifty to one hundred times.

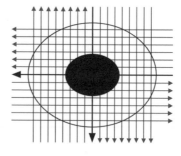

"THE CHI KNIFE HELPS ALL EYE PROBLEMS."

7. Do the same toward the left side; have the student move the eye to the left and slice with the Chi Knife toward the right.

8. When you feel that the Chi Knife is full of sick Chi, spiral counter-clockwise and discard it down to the ground. When you feel that the knife is emptied, charge it with Chi from the universe.

Other Energetic Surgery

The Chi Knife can be used to excise any problem in the body. It is especially good for soft tissue repair, including in the brain. Follow the same procedure

used on the eyes to carry out energetic surgery on any part of the anatomy.

The Chi Knife is also a powerful tool for use in breaking up stuck Chi that has manifested as a physical lump. If you are not sure exactly what you are working on (tumor, wart, or something else), focus on the area and say, either out loud or to yourself, "Chi Knife, please destroy all kinds of wounds, warts, and tumors." Cut up, down, and sideways in the cross pattern through the affected part.

"CHI KNIFE, PLEASE DESTROY ALL KINDS OF WOUNDS, WARTS, AND TUMORS."

STEP 3: ENERGIZE AND ACTIVATE THE IMMUNE SYSTEM

Step K of the general healing session outlines the techniques for energizing and activating the immune system. With enough practice, this exercise will become second nature. See page 174 to begin a review of this exercise.

STEP 4: CLEANSE THE INTERNAL ORGANS

This session can be used for any kind of ailment and carried out with any number of people, whether just the practitioner, the practitioner and one other person, a small group, or a large group. Greater energetic current is more likely to be created in larger groups. In the case of mass healings, a guide or conductor must open the channel for the others to follow. In the case of solo practice, the practitioner himself (or herself) will of course be the guide. The instructions given here are directed toward a practitioner working with a single student; they may be adapted for the practitioner working solo or with a group.

We recommend you spend about twenty minutes on the general healing session (see chapter 5) before moving on to the more specialized techniques of emptying and cleansing the body's centers, systems, and organs, as described in this chapter. We recommend that you spend between five and fifteen minutes on all of these specialized techniques. *Always* perform the Chi Water practice before undertaking the specialized practices in this chapter.

As an introduction to the organ cleansing process, in this chapter we'll focus on cleansing the solar plexus, spinal cord, blood (lungs), and circulation system (heart). These are among the major areas that commonly need cleansing.

It is important to remember that if your Tan Tien contains no energy, you will have no energy to work with. When you connect your center to the infinite source of the universe, the Tao, you access the power of the universe. Always hold on to your center; it is the only thing that is truly yours. Keep the Tan Tien Fire warm and spiraling. When you are aware of your Chi, you can direct heavenly light straight into your energy body and then into the student's.

General Cleansing Procedure

1. Push and pull the energy through the student's body. Push and disperse the sick energy into the universe and out to the planets, where it will be transformed and recycled.
2. Pull the energy back and stop it between yourself and the student.
3. Spiral the energy counterclockwise until you see the green light mix and clean the sick energy. Spiral and flush the energy down into the earth.
4. Spiral with blue light; see it mix and flush the energy within the student's body. Spiral this energy down to the ground.
5. Energize the student with white or violet light.

General Cleansing Principles

- Move your hand in a clockwise spiral to introduce energy to the body or to stabilize energy in the body.
- Move your hand in a counterclockwise spiral to clean, flush, and remove energy from the body. Afterward, sweep down the whole body to direct the sick energy into the earth.

- You can use both hands to channel Chi when you push and pull through the body.
- When it becomes necessary to switch from one color to another, an abrupt shaking movement of the hand should ensure a smooth transition.
- Pushing and pulling is like fanning and ventilating the body. Ventilation enables the stagnant, sick energy to leave the body.
- To energize means to draw Chi into the area that you want to receive healing. To cleanse means to push energy through the affected part and send it out to the universe, and then pull new Chi back into the same area. To stabilize means to restore normal function.
- The body's organs tend to store heat to differing degrees. In descending order (from those most likely to those least likely to store heat), the organs that store heat are the head, heart, liver, lungs, stomach and spleen, large intestine and small intestine, kidneys, and sexual organs (which become hot when aroused).
- When you begin pushing, pulling, and sweeping, you may feel resistance in the body. As you progress and the energy centers open, this feeling will diminish.
- Many color combinations can be applied to the various parts of the body. When you start practice, stick to the basic formula: first blue, then green, then white, then violet, and finally blue again. When you are working on a specific area, you can keep this book nearby to serve as a reminder of the correct order of colors, or you can write a short color "recipe" card for yourself before you begin. In this way, you will be able to relax your mind.
- To energize, use blue or white light.
- To cleanse, use green light.
- To flush, use blue light.
- To stabilize, use blue light.
- To balance sick energy and reprogram the cells of the body, use violet light.
- For general infections, use green light (to energize and clean), blue light (to stabilize), and violet light (to balance the sick energy and reprogram all the cells). Use the Chi Knife if necessary.
- Never use orange on the head, heart, or spleen.

Cleansing the Solar Plexus

The solar plexus acts as a distribuion center for emotional energy and is situated in between the lower and higher energy centers and in the center of most of the internal organs. All the organs dump their negative emotions in the solar plexus. Many people have an overheated solar plexus, which means that this area will require a lot of attention. You will feel the heat when you scan. The internal organs can be cleansed by a sweep of the solar plexus, in which you energize, cleanse, and flush it of negative energy.

1. You can cleanse the organs of the student's solar plexus by pushing and pulling Chi. Picture the organs and push; feel that your hands are very long, extending through the organs and reaching out to the universe. Use your intent to project all the sick energy down into the earth and out to the universe and the other planets of the solar system, where it will be processed and recycled. Pull the universal energy back toward yourself; when you pull the Chi back past the student, stop it in between you. Push and pull, push and pull, until you feel the energy or power of the universe flowing between you. Ask, "Give me the power to see." Feel your Chi entering the organs with ease.

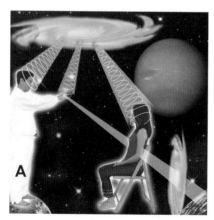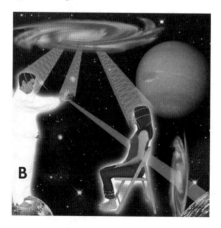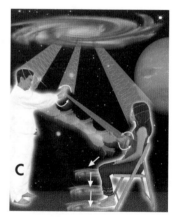

A. EXTEND THROUGH THE SOLAR PLEXUS AND REACH OUT TO THE UNIVERSE.
B. PUSH GREEN CHI THROUGH THE SOLAR PLEXUS, CONNECTING WITH THE UNIVERSE ON THE OTHER SIDE. C. PULL GREEN CHI THROUGH THE SOLAR PLEXUS, STOPPING IT WHEN IT COMES BETWEEN YOU. SPIRAL THE ENERGY CLOCKWISE INTO THE GROUND.

2. Push and pull green light through the solar plexus, spiraling counterclockwise. Feel the green light mixing with the sick energy. Talk to the sick energy; tell it to leave, and tell it you will take it to "a better place, where it will be happy. Give the command "Out." Push and pull until

you feel the energy in the solar plexus begin to disperse. Spiral the energy counterclockwise and guide it down to the ground.

3. Rinse and flush with blue light, spiraling it counterclockwise. Picture ocean blue in the solar plexus, and flush it down to the earth. See and feel the solar plexus becoming cleaner.

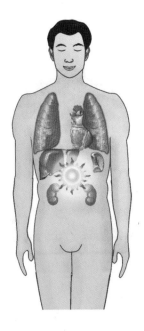

TO CLEANSE THE SOLAR PLEXUS, SPIRAL GREEN CHI COUNTERCLOCKWISE

FLUSH AND STABILIZE WITH BLUE CHI

4. Now flush out the whole body with blue and white Chi. With all the organs: from the lungs, heart, liver, gall bladder, pancreas, spleen, stomach, small intestine, large intestine, kidneys, and sexual organs. Clean all the way down to the earth. When you clean the solar plexus and all the other organs, you remove all the negative emotional energy.

5. Energize the spleen, liver, and kidneys with blue or white light. Then project green light, followed by orange light, to the core of the liver and kidneys. Clean these organs with the green and orange light. Then stabilize the organs with blue light.

6. Work on the back of the spleen. This organ helps clean the blood. Energize the spleen with blue-white light, spiraling the energy clockwise. See the spleen in your mideyebrow. See the cells and spiral the light into them. Give the command "Stay." This is very important; it

makes sure that none of the spleen cells hide from the dazzling light that you are sending. Give the command again. Then stabilize them with blue light.

7. Repeat step 6 with the kidneys.

8. Smile and laugh to the student's liver, and see all of its cells. Give the command "Stay." Then send in blue or white light (to energize), followed by green (to energize and clean), blue (to rinse and stabilize), violet (to recharge and reprogram), and then blue again.

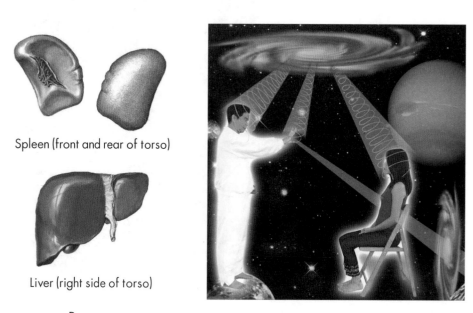

Spleen (front and rear of torso)

Liver (right side of torso)

PUSH AND PULL TO HELP DISPERSE THE ENERGY IN THE LIVER AND SPLEEN

It is essential that you feel and talk to any sick energy. If the student is healthy, you will feel his or her "light." Ask the student's energy body to tell you where it may need some healing. Send in "light radar." Transmit green light and flush down to the earth. When you feel energy accumulating, start to spiral more. Push and pull and give the command for the sick energy to leave.

The more you clean, the more you heal. Tell your student to practice at home after the session, at an agreed time. You can then carry out absent or distance healing, linking your own Personal Star and energy body with those of your student and with the universe. With time, you will master the techniques, imprinting them with your own manner. Eventually, as the blockages are cleared and the flow of Chi restored, the symptoms of sickness will disappear.

Cleansing the Spinal Cord

The spinal cord protects the entire body from diseased and negative energy, both physical and psychic. When you open the spinal cord and solar plexus, you can release many energy blockages.

1. Sweep the hand in a clockwise motion to energize the spine with blue, green, white, ultraviolet, or a combination thereof.
2. Spiral counterclockwise and brush the spine down to the ground.
3. Continue sweeping until you feel that the spinal cord has cooled down.

   Note: Do not use orange or red on the spinal cord.

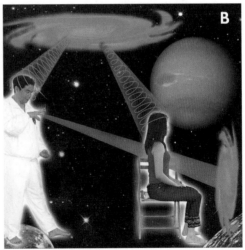

SPINAL CORD

Cleansing the Blood (Lungs)

Pale green-white and orange-white Chi work as cleansing agents for the blood. The blood requires cleansing on a regular basis, and this technique can also be used as treatment for diseases of the blood and arteries, as well as serious infections. The Chi first energizes the lungs; as the blood passes through the lungs, it takes in the Chi, thus becoming purified. The benefit is then carried to the rest of the body as the blood circulates. Note: This technique should not be used on pregnant women.

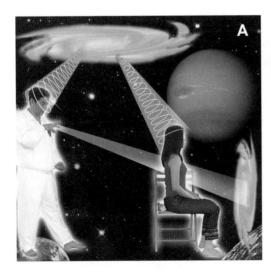

A. CLEANSING THE BLOOD AND EMPTYING THE LUNGS
B. BECOME AWARE OF YOUR THREE TAN TIENS. CONNECT TO THE UNIVERSE AND ASK FOR THE POWER TO SEE.

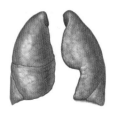

LUNGS

1. Scan the student.
2. Push through and open the lungs from the back to the front.
3. When the lungs need to be given energy, use pale green-white followed by pale orange-white Chi. Begin at the front and move to the rear. To make weak individuals stronger, red-white Chi can be employed; it will bring energy into the lungs.
4. Purification of the blood is carried out by the liver, kidneys, and spleen. Push and pull Chi through these organs.
5. Energize the liver, kidneys, and spleen with white Chi. Command the white Chi to remain in these organs. Fill yourself with the light.

Cleansing the Circulatory System and Heart

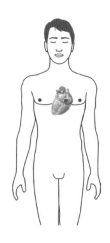

HEART

Having good blood is like running the highest quality motor oil through the engine of a motor vehicle. The sacrum and solar plexus are involved in the health of the circulatory system and heart. The sacrum controls the bones; indirectly, it stimulates bone marrow and enhances the quality of the blood. Within the Universal Tao system, the sacrum also is said to control the Chi pulse. If you have enough Chi, your heart does not have to work so hard, because the Chi pushes the blood.

The solar plexus, a center of emotional energy, affects the heart through two mechanisms:

- It may affect the heart directly, causing rhythmic disturbance or pressure around the heart muscle.
- Malfunction in the liver or digestive tract can lead to high cholesterol levels or gas, which pushes up toward the heart from the intestines and causes unwanted heat and pressure.

Cleansing the solar plexus will greatly improve these conditions. If you have been trained in Chi Nei Tsang, you can use it in combination with the Cosmic Healing techniques.

To support the heart muscle, take the following steps.

1. Clean out the solar plexus, as outlined earlier. Push and pull with green and blue Chi.
2. Detoxify the liver, flushing it with green Chi.
3. Enhance the treatment with white and violet light.

4. Use a finger to pass blue and white Chi through the lower left and upper right part of the heart. This small section frequently needs to be unblocked. Remember that the heart muscle is very delicate. You draw the force, you spiral, and you push.

5. Stabilize with white Chi. In cases of an enlarged heart, use blue.

6. Carefully use red Chi to balance the blood and open the blood vessels.

7. Sweep the sacrum with green, red, and blue Chi. You may choose to bring down one color at a time or blend threads of these colors together.

8. Sweep the solar plexus with green, blue, red, white, and violet Chi. You may choose to bring down one color at a time or blend threads of these colors together.

9. Energize and cool down the throat center, using blue.

HEALING SOME COMMON AILMENTS

The following descriptions are mere guidelines. Each case is different, and much depends on your own abilities. You need practice in order to be able to detect diseases. Best results with Cosmic Healing will be obtained when it is practiced in combination with Chi Nei Tsang.

Remember that these techniques are not meant to replace medical care but merely to assist it. Also, the student must always work with the practitioner; the practitioner is a channel, the student the healer.

Hypertension (High Blood Pressure)

Overactive adrenals or kidneys often cause hypertension. The basic problem is that Chi goes up but cannot come down.

1. Clean out the solar plexus first. The solar plexus links to the eleventh thoracic vertebra (T11), which has a direct nerve effect on the adrenal glands. The adrenal glands produce adrenaline, the hormone that stimulates the heart to pump. Overactive adrenal glands will eventually affect the heart.

2. Tune up the Door of Life with blue Chi, calming it.

3. Take the pressure from the heart by flushing it with green Chi.

4. Energize the heart using violet Chi.

5. The basic problem with hypertension is that the Chi goes up but cannot come down. Flush down the body from head to feet using blue Chi.
6. Work on the sacrum, using orange and yellow Chi.

Hypotension (Low Blood Pressure)

In hypotension the Door of Life and the adrenal glands are underactive.

1. First clean out the solar plexus, this time focusing on removing blocks or stuck energy.
2. Energize the Door of Life, using green and red Chi.
3. Energize the sacrum, again using green and red Chi.
4. Energize the base of skull with green and violet Chi.

Stomach Pains

1. Scan the student.
2. Sweep the abdominal area, paying particular attention to the solar plexus, navel, and lower abdomen.
3. Apply green and blue Chi to the navel.
4. Use blue Chi to stabilize the energy.

If the stomach pains persist, treat with Chi Nei Tsang or seek the advice of a qualified medical practitioner.

General Pain

Blue Chi has a calming effect and relieves pain. Green Chi frees and expels disease energy.

1. Push and pull the energy through the affected area out to the universe, or ground the sick energy until partial relief is attained.
2. Energize the affected area with pale green-white Chi and with a large amount of pale blue-white.

Another method for eliminating pain is to switch back and forth between pale green-white Chi and pale orange-white Chi.

Headache

1. Scan the eyes, temple, crown, mideyebrow, forehead, back of the head and neck, spine, and solar plexus to check for congestion or depletion.
2. If eyestrain is the cause of the headache, sweep down the eye and temple bones and flush them down to the ground.
3. Sweep the whole head, particularly the painful area.
4. Energize the area with pale green-white, blue-white, and pale violet-white Chi. You may choose to bring down one color at a time or blend threads of these colors together.

Migraine Headache

Persons who suffer from prolonged or chronic headaches, including migraines, have an abnormal accumulation of energy in various parts of their bodies, particularly the solar plexus. This congestion follows a route up the vertebral column and into the neck and head. As a result, the various blood vessels in the head expand, causing pain in the head area. Mental strain, stress, and emotional disturbances usually cause this type of headache.

1. Use a pushing movement to cleanse and open the solar plexus and liver. Energize the solar plexus with first pale green-white, then pale blue-white, and finally mauve-white Chi.
2. Sweep the spine and send the sick red Chi into the ground.
3. Push through the back of the heart in order to open it and remove the dirty Chi. Then energize the heart with pale green-white and purple Chi. Use your mind to see the heart center expanding and opening.
4. Sweep the whole head and send the dirty Chi to the earth.
5. Use a combination of pale green-white, blue, and purple Chi to energize the back of the head, the crown, the mideyebrow, and the forehead.

Toothache

1. Sweep the area with pale green-white Chi.
2. Energize the area with pale green-white, mauve-white, and blue Chi. You may choose to bring down one color at a time or blend threads of these colors together.

Broken Bone

For any ailment relating to the bones, always activate the sacrum. Light orange-yellow Chi is used to encourage fractures to knit quickly. The sacrum attracts the orange-yellow Chi; feel the eight holes in the bone breathing. The orange-yellow Chi enters, transfers up to the crown, and is sent up to the universe to multiply.

1. Sweep the area of the fracture with pale green-white and pale orange-white Chi.
2. Energize the area of the fracture with pale orange-yellow Chi mixed with white. Visualize the core of the light (about 70 percent of it) as being luminous white; the outer layers are split equally between yellow and orange.
3. Push through and sweep the sacrum and navel using light red Chi mixed with white.
4. Repeat the healing every day.

Back Injury

1. Scan the student to see which parts are congested.
2. Sweep the spine and the area where the trauma is located with first pale white-green Chi and then pale white-orange Chi.
3. Energize the damaged area with a combination of pale blue-white, green, and purple Chi.
4. Sweep the back and front of the solar plexus with white Chi.
5. Stabilize the Chi in the damaged area by instructing it to be healthy and balanced.

Infection and Inflammation

1. Sweep the affected area with green and orange-white Chi. For the heart and spleen, these colors should be replaced with green and purple.
2. Energize the area with white, orange, green, blue, and light violet. This will strengthen the natural immune powers of the body.

Cysts

During the course of the session, scan and rescan the student's body. It is sometimes necessary to sweep as many as two hundred times to cool the affected area. Scanning will enable you to take a temperature reading. If the area is still hot, continue sweeping until it reaches a satisfactory temperature.

1. Push and pull green and blue Chi through the solar plexus area.
2. Use the Chi Knife to remove the cyst. Spiral clockwise with green and orange Chi, moving the "stuck" red Chi out of the body and grounding it in the earth.
3. Use blue Chi to stabilize and calm. Green and orange may be used to provide energy.
4. Repeat the healing three times a week.

Because spicy foods carry a lot of red Chi, the student should minimize his or her intake of them. The student should also practice the Cosmic Inner Smile to calm and balance his or her emotional state.

Fever

Have the student lie down to receive the healing. (In all cases where the student is unable to sit up comfortably, he or she may lie down.)

1. Sweep the body with blue or green Chi.
2. Push and pull through the affected part, sweeping the spleen with green and blue Chi. Clean and rinse thoroughly.
3. Apply blue and orange Chi to the solar plexus area. (Don't use orange if the student has diarrhea.)
4. Push and pull on the back of the heart and thymus to help fight off the infection. Sweep the heart with green and blue Chi. Then energize with green, orange, and violet Chi, which will stimulate the thymus gland.
5. Sweep both lungs. Energize the back of the lung area with orange and green Chi.
6. Sweep the spleen with green Chi.

Insomnia

Inability to sleep may be caused by overactivity in the solar plexus or overactivity and congestion in the sacrum. Similar problems can also occur in the throat, mideyebrow, crown, and forehead. Scan and rescan as the treatment progresses.

1. Push and pull until you feel the affected areas open.
2. Cleanse the sacrum and solar plexus with green and blue Chi.
3. Use blue Chi to soothe the solar plexus and induce sleep.
4. Sweep the mideyebrow, forehead, and crown with blue and green Chi.
5. Sweep the navel with white and orange Chi.
6. Stabilize with blue.

You can also recommend to the student that he or she not eat food late in the evening. The student may also wish to sleep in a separate bed from his or her partner; even two beds pushed next to each other may help.

Tinnitus

This condition relates to weakened kidneys. Work on the kidneys, mideyebrow, and forehead. Be sure to spend plenty of time flushing with blue.

Fresh Burns

Because of the cooling and calming properties of blue Chi, it can be used to remove the heat from burns. Green has a similar effect.

1. Scan the affected area.
2. Sweep the affected area with a combination of pale green-white and blue Chi.
3. Energize the affected area with light green-white and blue Chi.
4. Continue to sweep and energize until relief is felt and the heat is released.

Old Minor Burns

1. Scan the affected area. (Rescan repeatedly during the session.)
2. Sweep the affected area with pale green-white and orange Chi. (Avoid the head and sensitive organs such as the eyes and brain.)

3. To energize and soothe the affected area, apply pale blue-white Chi. For rapid healing, apply green and light red, in equal proportions; this mixture optimizes the breakdown of necrotic cellular material. (If you are working near the head, use light violet-white instead of red.)
4. Sweep the sacrum and the navel with light red-white Chi.
5. Stabilize the area with blue Chi, which also assists in the release of the stagnant Chi.
6. Repeat the healing session for two or three days.

Old Severe Burns

1. Scan the student at the beginning and end of the treatment.
2. Sweep the affected area, alternating between pale green-white Chi and pale orange-white Chi. Avoid sensitive organs and the head area.
3. To speed up healing and reduce pain and infection, energize the affected area with pale blue-white, pale green-white, and mauve-white Chi.
4. For rapid healing, after a few days have passed and the pain has lessened considerably, energize the affected area with pale green-white and pale red-white Chi. (If you are working on the head, use mauve mixed with white in place of the red.)
5. Sweep the sacrum and navel. To speed up healing, energize the area with white Chi.
6. Make your healing intent stable by telling the body and the universe to continue the healing process, without your assistance, until balance has been achieved.

Old Wounds

Do not use green Chi on open wounds because it works slowly and tends to make the wound moist and runny. Green Chi is quite effective, however, for treating old wounds. A large amount of green Chi is necessary to break down dead cells.

1. Scan at the beginning and end of the treatment.
2. Sweep the affected area with pale green-white and pale orange-white Chi.
3. Energize the affected area with a little pale blue-white Chi.
4. Energize the affected area with equal amounts of pale green-white Chi and then pale red-white Chi. This treatment can speed up the healing process and assist in the breakdown of cellular material.

5. To accelerate the healing, sweep the navel and sacrum and vitalize them with pale red-white Chi.
6. Make your healing intent stable by telling the body and the universe to continue the healing process, without your assistance, until balance has been achieved.

Skin Infection

The skin is related to the lungs and the kidneys. In all cases of skin infection, the immune system is involved.

1. Enhance immunity as outlined on pages 174–185.
2. Focus on strengthening the lungs. Always start with green to flush out. Then send orange light into the lungs. (Make sure you are not sending it up to the brain.) Energize the lungs with blue and white.
3. Detoxify the kidneys, purifying the blood with green and energizing with blue. Ask the student to visualize a fresh mountain stream to stimulate the kidneys.
4. Treat the area locally, using your hands. If the area is big, use your palm; if it is small, use your fingers. Do not focus on your palms (see "Forget about Your Palms" on pages 95–96). Draw green Chi from the forest, and then energize with violet.
5. To diminish pain or itchiness, use blue to cool down. Also use the Chi knife to work on the infection.

If the skin problem is allergy-based, you should also treat the mideyebrow; there might be some irritation here. First clean with green, then either energize with violet (if resistance is low) or soothe with a light shade of yellow.

If the skin problem is related to asthma, open the lungs with bright red, clean the throat center with green, and energize the throat center with deep blue.

If the problem is due to toxicity, clean out the liver, flushing it with a combination of green and orange. Energize with green. Enhance the immune system by working on the sacrum.

Eye Problems

The right eye is governed by the forehead, and the left eye by the mideyebrow. The eyes are also linked to the temples.

1. Ask the student to touch his or her temple bone, and guide him or her in taking in the white or light violet Chi.
2. Send the Chi all the way through the mideyebrow and forehead. Ask the student to visualize the light coming in. Use soft shades of green with golden yellow to stimulate the optic nerve. Use blue to calm the eye muscles and light violet to stimulate the inner eyesight.
3. The eyes are connected to the liver. Scan the liver and energize with green.
4. Scan the jawbone to see if there is any unreleased anger. Cool down with blue.
5. Channel bright green into the liver.

Ear Infection

The right ear is governed by the forehead and the left ear by the mideyebrow.
1. Flush the ear with blue Chi to cool it in case there is an infection.
2. Push and pull green Chi to clean the ears.
3. The ears are connected to the kidneys, so work on them next.
4. The ears are also connected to the sinuses and upper respiratory tract. When infection is present, use blue to cool these areas and violet to clean and energize.

Improve Health, Reduce Stress, and Remain Young

1. Sweep the solar plexus, liver, stomach, and pancreas.
2. Energize the crown, forehead, back of the head, and left and right brain with white Chi.
3. Energize the front and rear of the heart and lungs with white-purple Chi.
4. Energize the front and rear of the spleen, the navel and lower abdominal area, the spinal cord, and the kidneys with white Chi.
5. Energize the sexual center with white Chi. If a problem in this area is difficult to shift, use green Chi instead.
6. Energize the sacrum with white Chi.
7. Energize the other organs with green or purple Chi.
8. Energize the arms and hands with white Chi and the legs and feet with white-purple Chi.
9. Energize the eyes with green-yellow Chi.
10. After a session with people who are particularly weak, apply pale blue-white Chi to stabilize and instruct them not to bathe for one full day.

Appendix
Guide to the Acupuncture Points
Used in Cosmic Chi Kung

The following is a detailed description of the acupuncture energy points used in the Cosmic Healing Chi Kung practice. It is necessary to know the exact location of the points to do the practice well. However, you do not have to know the traditional Chinese medical functions and energetics of the points to do the practice. These are included in this appendix as an item of interest.

The names of the points are given first by the channel and number, second by the English translation of the traditional Chinese name for the point, and finally by the name in Chinese.

We are emphasizing the traditional Chinese medical therapeutic properties of the points given herein. Many of these points have very different purposes in Taoist Yoga. For a description of the Taoist Yoga energetics, refer to *Awaken Healing Light of the Tao* by Mantak Chia.

PERICARDIUM 8

Lakor's Palace/Laogong

Ying Spring, Fire Point

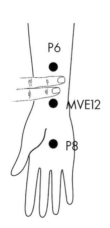

Location: On the center of the palm, where the tip of the middle finger touches when making a loose fist.

Functions: Cools the heart, drains heat from the heart, cools the blood, calms the spirit, regulates the Chi and yang of the heart, Ghost Point for treating spirit possession.

Indications: Coma from stroke, heat exhaustion, angina pectoris, mania, hysteria, mental illness, excessive sweating of the palms, mouth problems.

LARGE INTESTINE 4

Adjoining Valleys/Hegu

Yuan Source Point

Location: On the back side of the hand between the thumb and index finger, in the web approximately at the middle of the metacarpal bone of the index finger.

Functions: Disperses wind, relieves exterior conditions, suppresses pain, clears the channels, clears lung heat, calms the spirit.

Very powerful point for moving the Chi and blood of the whole body; main point for pain; main point for headache; main point for ailments of the head, face, and sensory organs; main point for immunity.

Indications: Headaches, common cold, redness with pain and swelling of the eyes, toothache, facial swelling, sore throat, finger cramps, arm pain, fever, abdominal pain, constipation.

Caution: Contraindicated in pregnancy.

SMALL INTESTINE 3

Back Creek/Houxi

Shu Stream, Wood Point
Master Point of the Governor Channel
Coupled Point of the Yang Bridge Channel

Location: When a loose fist is made, the point is near the head of the fifth metacarpal bone on the knife edge of the hand at the junction of the red and white skin.

Functions: Relaxes the tendon-muscular channels, opens the Governor Channel, clears the Spirit, drains evil Chi from the heart.

Indications: Seizures; psychosis; hysteria; intercostal neuralgia; headache; stiff neck; red, painful, and congested eyes; deafness; spasms of the arm, elbow and fingers; fever; night sweating; whiplash; occipital headaches.

Used for structural/musculoskeletal problems; opens the Governor Channel for problems with back, neck, and head, main point for stiff neck; antispasmodic for muscle spasms; anti-inflammatory for spinal arthritis and intestinal inflammation.

LUNG 10

Fish Border/Yuji

Ying Spring, Fire Point

L10

Location: In the middle of the ulna eminence below the thumbs at the junction of the red and white skin.

Functions: Cools heat in the lungs, benefits the throat.

Indications: Sore throat, cough, laryngitis, tonsillitis, fever with common cold.

TRIPLE WARMER 5

Outer Gate/Wai Guan

Luo Connecting Point
Master Point of the Yang Regulator Channel
Coupled Point of the Belt Channel

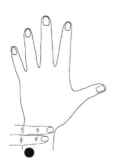

TW5

Location: About two fingers' width above the wrist crease on the outside of the arm.

Functions: Regulates the Yang Regulator Channel and Belt Channel, tonifies and consolidates protective (Wei) Chi, releases exterior hot and cold conditions, helps circulate stagnant Chi in the channels.

Indications: Common cold with alternating chills and fever, high fevers, pneumonia, deafness, migraine headaches, paralysis, stiff neck.

PERICARDIUM 6

Inner Gate/Nei Guan

Luo Connecting Point
Master Point of the Yin Regulator Channel

Location: About two fingers' width above the wrist crease on the inside of the arm, between the two prominent tendons.

Functions: Calms the heart and spirit, regulates the Chi, opens and relaxes the chest, regulates and harmonizes the stomach, regulates the liver, relieves pain.

Indications: Rheumatic heart disease, shock, angina pectoris, palpitations, chest pain, asthma, shortness of breath, tightness or fullness in the chest, spasm of the diaphragm, vomiting, stomachache, abdominal pain, morning sickness, motion sickness, migraine headaches, hysteria, anxiety, irritability, insomnia, seizures, swollen and painful throat, painful menses, nausea with menses.

LARGE INTESTINE 11

Crooked Pond/Qu Chi

He Sea, Earth Point
Ghost Point

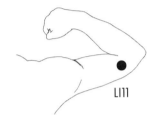

Location: When the elbow is flexed, in the depression at the outer and upper end of the elbow crease.
Functions: Cools heat, clears fire, drains dampness, eliminates wind and exterior conditions, regulates and moistens large intestine.
Indications: Arthritic pain in the arms, paralysis, hypertension, high fever, anemia, allergies, skin problems, Parkinson's disease.

Main point for skin diseases; main point for high fever.

CONCEPTION VESSEL 22

Heaven's Chimney/Tian Tu

Intersecting Point of the Yin Regulator Channel on the Conception Vessel
Window of the Sky Point

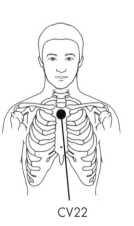

Location: At the top of the breastbone (sternum) in the V-shaped indentation (suprasternal notch). Press in and downward at a forty-five-degree angle.
Functions: Cools the throat and clears the voice, facilitates and regulates movement of lung Chi, frees the breath and helps restore the proper functioning of the lungs and bronchi, helps open Conception Vessel (Functional Channel).
Indications: Asthma, bronchial asthma, bronchitis, coughing, pharyngitis, goiter, hiccups, nervous vomiting, hoarse voice, spasms of the esophagus, diseases of the vocal cords, sore throat.

CONCEPTION VESSEL 17

Central Altar/Tan Zhong

Front Mu-Alarm Point of the pericardium, Influential Point of Chi of the body Sea of Chi Point, Master Point of the Middle Tan Tien

Location: On the frontal midline at the level of the fourth intercostal space, between the nipples.

Functions: Regulates the lungs and the Upper Warmer, tonifies Ancestral Chi, opens and relaxes the chest, diffuses lung Chi, regulates and tonifies Chi, transforms phlegm.

Indications: Pulmonary tuberculosis with shortness of breath, bronchitis, asthma, bronchial asthma, chest pain, wheezing, labored breathing, palpitations, difficulty swallowing food, anxiety. All breast problems such as mastitis, insufficient lactation, breast abscesses.

CONCEPTION VESSEL 12

Middle Cavity/Zhongwan (Solar Plexus)

Front Mu-Alarm Point of the stomach, Influential point of all yang organs

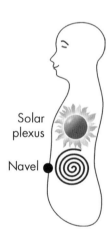

Solar plexus

Navel

Location: Approximately midway between the navel and the top joint of the xiphoid process.

Functions: Regulates the stomach Chi and yin, regulates, strengthens and tonifies the spleen Chi and yang, regulates the Middle Warmer, reduces digestive stagnation, tonifies nutritive Chi, regulates Chi and blood, redirects rebellious Chi downward, clears stomach fire and heat, calms the fetus, controls the aura.

Indications: Acute or chronic gastritis, stomach and duodenal ulcers, prolapsed stomach, acute intestinal obstruction, stomachache, vomiting, abdominal distention, diarrhea, constipation, acid regurgitation, indigestion, hypertension, mental diseases.

MIDEYEBROW POINT

Seal Hall/Yin Tang

Master Point of the Upper Tan Tien

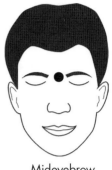

Location: At the midpoint between the two eyebrows.
Functions: Calms the spirit, activates the Crystal Room, opens the Governor Channel, draws in Cosmic Chi, eliminates wind heat.
Indications: Headache, vertigo, rhinitis, sinusitis, common cold, hypertension, infantile convulsions, sore eyes.

Mideyebrow point

CONCEPTION VESSEL 6

Chi Ocean/Chi Hai

Master Point of the Lower Tan Tien

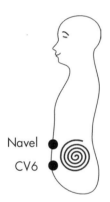

Location: Approximately three fingers' width below the navel.
Functions: Regulates Chi, tonifies Original Chi, strengthens weak kidneys, harmonizes the blood, regulates the Thrusting Route Conception Vessel, reinforces Ching Chi, enriches yin.
Indications: Neurasthenia, abdominal distention, abdominal pain, irregular menstruation, impotence, spermatorrhea, urinary retention, frequent urination, intestinal paralysis, incontinence, constipation, infertility, uterine bleeding, hernia.

Navel
CV6

STOMACH 13

Chi's Household/Chi Hu

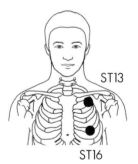

Location: Below the midpoint of the collarbone along the mammillary line (directly above the nipple).
Functions: Clears heat, loosens the chest, relaxes the diaphragm, regulates lung Chi.
Indications: Asthma, bronchitis, chest and back pain, hiccups.

ST13
ST16

STOMACH 16

Breast's Window/Ying Chuang

Location: In the space between the third and fourth ribs, one rib directly above the nipple in men, slightly higher in women.

Functions: Stops pain, reduces swelling, clears heat, resolves depression, opens lungs, stops cough, relaxes chest, moves Chi.

Indications: Coughing, asthma, swelling of the breasts, chest and stomach pain, heartburn, shortness of breath, melancholy, diarrhea.

LIVER 14

Gate of Hope/Chi Men

Front Mu-Alarm Point of the liver
Intersecting point of the Yin
Regulator and spleen channels on the liver channel

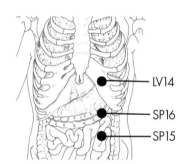

Location: In the sixth intercostal space, directly below the nipple.

Functions: Spreads liver Chi, transforms and removes congealed blood, strengthens spleen and stomach, expands and relaxes the chest.

Indications: Difficulty in breathing, chest pain, hepatitis, enlarged liver, gallstones, pleurisy, nervous stomach, menopausal disorders, cholera, failure to discharge the placenta after childbirth.

SPLEEN 16

Abdomen's Sorrow/Fu Ai

Location: Just below the bottom edge of the rib cage on the mammillary line.

Functions: Frees bowel Chi, dispels damp and heat, opens the organs and clears Chi stagnation.

Indications: Pain in the navel region, indigestion, dysentary, constipation.

SPLEEN 15

Great Horizontal/Da Heng

Intersecting point of the Yin Regulator Channel on the spleen channel

Location: At the level with the navel along the mammillary line.

Functions: Regulates the spleen, regulates and moistens the intestines, reduces digestive stagnation and transforms damp heat.

Indications: Abdominal distension, diarrhea, constipation, intestinal paralysis, parasitic worms in the intestines, chronic sadness.

CONCEPTION VESSEL 8

Spirit Palace Gate/Shen Que

Doorway to the Original Chi

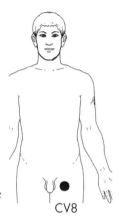

Location: In the center of the navel

Functions: Tonifies, strengthens, and regulates the Chi and yang of the spleen and the Chi of the stomach, regulates the intestines, warms the interior and reduces digestive stagnation, tonifies the kidneys, warms the yang, dries dampness and dispels cold.

Indications: Chronic diarrhea, intestinal tuberculosis, all urinary disorders, shock resulting from intestinal adhesions, heatstroke, rectal or anal prolapse, restless fetus.

GOVERNOR VESSEL 4

Door of Life/Ming Men

Back Doorway to the Lower Tan Tien

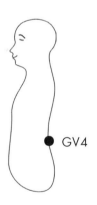

Location: Below the spinous process of the second lumbar vertebrae. Approximately at the level of the navel.

Functions: Nourishes the Original Chi, strengthens and harmonizes the kidneys, tonifies ching and yang, clears channels and invigorates collateral vessels, benefits the lower back and bones, regulates water pathways. Main point to build life fire; main point for sexual/genital problems.

Indications: Bone disorders, chronic nephritis, enuresis, low sex drive, fatigue, spermatorrhea, impotence, irregular menses, painful menses, no menses, scanty menses, abnormal uterine bleeding, lower back stiffness and pain, kidney pain radiating to the abdomen, hemorrhoids, urinary incontinence, painful urination, diarrhea, sciatica, spinal myelitis.

GOVERNOR VESSEL 6

Middle of Spine/Jizhong

Location: Below the spinous process of the eleventh thoracic vertebra (T11).
Functions: Stimulates Ching Chi, benefits spleen, stomach, kidneys, and liver.
Indications: Hepatitis, seizures, low back pain, paralysis of lower limbs, blood in stools, diabetes, diarrhea.

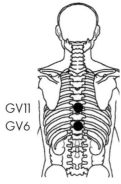

GV11
GV6

GOVERNOR VESSEL 11

Spirit's Path/Shen Tao

Location: Below the spinous process of T5 (opposite CV17, the Heart Point).
Functions: Calms heart and mind, regulates heart Chi and yang, expands and relaxes the chest, benefits heart and lungs, sedates pain, sedates fright and dispels wind.
Indications: Anxiety and palpitations due to fear or fright, neurasthenia, asthma, cough, shortness of breath, chest and hypochondriac pain, insomnia, aphasia due to winds, stroke, forgetfulness, fever.

GOVERNOR VESSEL 14

Big Vertebra/Da Zhui

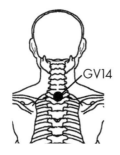

GV14

Influential point of yang
Sea of Chi point
Intersection point of all yang channels.

Location: Below the spinous process of the seventh cervical vertebra (C7), approximately at the level of the shoulders.
Functions: Opens the yang, clears the brain, calms the spirit, tonifies protective (Wei) Chi, reduces fever, relieves exterior conditions, clears heat.
Indications: Fever, sunstroke, malaria, psychosis, seizures, bronchitis, asthma, pulmonary tuberculosis, emphysema, hepatitis, blood diseases, eczema, hemiplegia, pain in the back of the shoulders, cold-induced diseases, cough, fever and chills.

GOVERNOR VESSEL 16

Jade Pillow/Feng Fu

Sea of Marrow Point, Window of Sky Point, Ghost Point
Intersection point of the Yang Regulator Channel on the Governor Vessel

Location: At the base of the skull, about one inch above the posterior hairline.

Functions: Benefits and clears the brain, calms spirit, opens the sensory orifices, dispels wind, smooths joint functions.

Indications: Seizures, mania, hemiplegia, loss of speech due to stroke, delirium, suicidal behavior, fear and fright, anxiety, common cold, sensation of heaviness in the head, headache, dizziness, numbness of the limbs, deaf-mutism, blurred vision, sinusitis, stiff neck.

GOVERNOR VESSEL 20

One Hundred Meetings/Bai Hui

Sea of Marrow Point

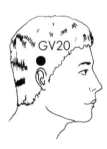

Location: At the crown of the head, approximately on the midpoint of the line connecting the top apex of the two ears.

Function: Clears the senses, calms the spirit, extinguishes liver wind, stabilizes ascending yang.

Indications: Headache, dizziness, shock, depression, hypertension, insomnia, seizures, prolapsed anus, prolapsed uterus, mental dullness, hemorrhoids.

Bibliography

Chia, Mantak. *Awaken Healing Light of the Tao.* Huntington, NY: Healing Tao Books, 1993.

———. *Chi Nei Tsang: Internal Organ Chi Massage.* Huntington, NY: Healing Tao Books, 1990.

———. *Healing Love through the Tao: Cultivating Female Sexual Energy.* Huntington, NY: Healing Tao Books, 1986.

———. *Taoist Secrets of Love: Cultivating Male Sexual Energy.* New York: Aurora Press, 1984.

"Complex and Hidden Brain in the Gut Makes Stomachaches and Butterflies." *The New York Times,* section C1, January 23, 1996.

Cooper, Geoffrey M. *The Cell: A Molecular Approach.* Washington, DC: Sinauer Associates, 1996.

DeLaney, Colleen, David Leonard, and Lancelot Kitsch. *The Acupuncture Point Book.* Santa Cruz, CA: Roast Duck Productions, 1989.

Dinshah, Darius. *Let There Be Light.* Malaga, N. J.: Dinshah Health Society, 1985.

Dong, Paul, and Aristide H. Esser. *Chi Gong: The Ancient Chinese Way to Health.* New York: Paragon House, 1990.

Fox, Stuart Ira. *Human Physiology.* Boston: McGraw-Hill, 1999.

Gershon, Michael D. *The Second Brain.* New York: HarperCollinsPublishers, 1998.

Jou, Tsung Hwa. *The Tao of Meditation: Way to Enlightenment.* Piscataway, NJ: Tai Chi Foundation, 1983.

Lade, Arnie. *Acupuncture Points: Images and Functions.* Seattle, WA: Eastland Press, 1989.

Lindsay, Mary. *The Visual Dictionary of the Human Body.* First American edition. New York: Dorling Kindersley Publications, 1991.

Lorenzen, Lee H. *Message from Water: Word of Recommendation.* 1984.

Lu, Kuan Yu. *Taoist Yoga: Alchemy and Immortality.* New York: Samuel Weiser, 1970.

Maciocia, Giovanni. *The Foundations of Chinese Medicine.* Edinburgh: Churchill Livingstone, 1989.

Matsumoto, Kiiko, and Stephen Birch. *Extraordinary Vessels.* Brookline, MA: Paradigm Publications, 1986.

Morrison, Philip and Phylis, and the Office of Charles and Ray Eames. *Power of Ten*. New York: Scientific American Books, 1982.

Nilsson, Lennart and Jan Lindberg. *The Body Victorious.* New York: Delacorte Press, 1985.

Pearsall, Paul. *The Heart's Code.* New York: Broadway Books, 1998.

Shanghai College of Traditional Medicine. *Acupuncture: A Comprehensive Text.* Translated by John O'Connor and Dan Bensky. Seattle, WA: Eastland Press, 1981.

Sui, Choa Kok. *Advanced Pranic Healing.* York Beach, Me.: S. Weiser, 1995.

Teeguarden, Iona Marsaa. *Acupressure Way of Health: Jin Shin Do.* Tokyo: Japan Publications, 1978.

Tortora, Gerard J., and Sandra R. Grabowski. *Introduction to the Human Body: The Essentials of Anatomy and Physiology.* Fifth edition. New York: Wiley, 2001.

Yang, Jwing-Ming. *The Root of Chinese Chi Kung.* Jamaica Plains, MA: YMAA, 1989.

About the Author

Mantak Chia has been studying the Taoist approach to life since childhood. His mastery of this ancient knowledge, enhanced by his study of other disciplines, has resulted in the development of the Universal Tao System, which is now being taught throughout the world.

Mantak Chia was born in Thailand to Chinese parents in 1944. When he was six years old, he learned from Buddhist monks how to sit and "still the mind." While in grammar school he learned traditional Thai boxing and soon went on to acquire considerable skill in Aikido, Yoga, and Tai Chi. His studies of the Taoist way of life began in earnest when he was a student in Hong Kong, ultimately leading to his mastery of a wide variety of esoteric disciplines. To better understand the mechanisms behind healing energy, he also studied Western anatomy and medical sciences.

Master Chia has taught his system of healing and energizing practices to tens of thousands of students and trained more than two thousand instructors and practitioners throughout the world. He has established centers for Taoist study and training in many countries around the globe. In June 1990 he was honored by the International Congress of Chinese Medicine and Qigong (Chi Kung), which named him the Qigong Master of the Year.

The Universal Tao System and Training Center

THE UNIVERSAL TAO SYSTEM

The ultimate goal of Taoist practice is to transcend physical boundaries through the development of the soul and the spirit within the human. That is also the guiding principle behind the Universal Tao, a practical system of self-development that enables individuals to complete the harmonious evolution of their physical, mental, and spiritual bodies. Through a series of ancient Chinese meditative and internal energy exercises, the practitioner learns to increase physical energy, release tension, improve health, practice self-defense, and gain the ability to heal oneself and others. In the process of creating a solid foundation of health and well-being in the physical body, the practitioner also creates the basis for developing his or her spiritual potential by learning to tap into the natural energies of the Sun, Moon, Earth, Stars and other environmental forces.

The Universal Tao practices are derived from ancient techniques rooted in the processes of nature. They have been gathered and integrated into a coherent, accessible system for well-being that works directly with the life force, "Chi," flowing through the meridian system of the body.

Master Chia has spent years developing and perfecting techniques for passing these traditional practices to students around the world through ongoing classes, workshops, private instruction and healing sessions, as well as books and video and audio products. Further information can be obtained at www.universal-tao.com.

UNIVERSAL TAO CENTER

The Tao Garden Resort and Training Center in northern Thailand is the home of Master Chia and serves as the worldwide headquarters for Universal Tao activities. This integrated wellness, holistic health, and training center is situated on eighty acres surrounded by the beautiful Himalayan foothills near the historic walled city of Chiang Mai. The serene setting includes flower and herb gardens ideal for meditation, open-air Simple Chi Kung pavilions, and a health and fitness spa.

The Center offers classes year-round, as well as summer and winter retreats. It can accommodate 200 students, and group leasing can be arranged. For more information, you may fax the Center at (66)(53) 495-852, or email universaltao@universal-tao.com.

 Index

Italic page numbers indicate illustrations.

described, 2, 3, 221–22
foundations of, 5, 8–9
Web site, 5, 221
universe, connecting with, 42
upper brain. *See* Upper Tan
	Tien
upper palate, *95*
Upper Tan Tien
	described, *46*
	energy used by, 39
	increasing Chi in, 39–40, 41
	opening, 60–62
	second brain and, 36

violet light
	charging with, 165–73
	described, 75–76
	electric violet, 75, 76
	healing with, 170, 171, 172
viruses, 72, 177

warming up the stove, 9–10
warm-up exercises
	rotating the sacrum, 43, 44

shaking, 44–45
spinal cord breathing, 43–44
See also self-preparation
warts, 191
water
	polluted, 151
	sacred, 149–58
Wei Chi (Defensive Chi), 84
white light
	described, 72
	as Earth Chi, 71
	lungs healed with,
		12–13
	as solar Chi, 70
	spleen and, 81
womb, 57
World Link, 143–44
worry, 21, 39, 138
wounds, 205–6
Wu Chi (Place of Nothingness), 165

yang channels, 91–92, 126–27
yang energy
	described, 44

excess, 89
Governor Channel as, 90
healing with, 189
meridians and, 84
*Yellow Emperor's Classic of Internal
	Medicine, The*, 85
yellow light, 13, 22, 71, 75
yin and yang palms, 106–7, 112,
	118
yin channels, 89, 91–92, 124–25,
	126–27
yin energy
	described, 44, 156, 189
	earth energy as, 97
	excess, 89, 90
	Functional Channel and, 90
	meridans and, 84
	Sacred Water and, 156
Yi power
	activating, 98, 139–40
	overview, 7–8, 45, *46*, *145*
youthfulness, 207